Preaching and Teaching from the Old Testament

A Guide for the Church

Walter C. Kaiser Jr.

Baker Academic

A Division of Baker Book House Co
Grand Rapids, Michigan 49516

Published by Baker Academic
a division of Baker Book House Company
P.O. Box 6287, Grand Rapids, MI 49516-6287
www.bakeracademic.com

Third printing, June 2004

Printed in the United States of America

Library of Congress Cataloging-in-Publication Data
Kaiser, Walter C.
    Preaching and teaching from the Old Testament : a guide for the church / Walter C. Kaiser, Jr.
        p.   cm.
    Includes bibliographical references (p.) and indexes.
    ISBN 0-8010-2610-5 (pbk.)
    1. Bible. O.T.—Homiletical use. 2. Preaching. I. Title
BS1191.5 .K35 2003
221'.0071—dc21   2002035608

Dedicated to

Dr. Carl F. H. Henry
and his wife, Helga

Two of God's choicest servants
and friends in the work of the gospel

Contents

Introduction   9

Part 1   The Need to Preach and Teach from the Old Testament

1. The Value of the Old Testament for Today   15
2. The Problem of the Old Testament for Today   29
3. The Task of Preaching and Teaching from the Old Testament Today   39
4. The Art and Science of Expository Preaching   49

Part 2   How to Preach and Teach from the Old Testament

5. Preaching and Teaching Narrative Texts of the Old Testament   63
6. Preaching and Teaching the Wisdom Books of the Old Testament   83
7. Preaching and Teaching the Prophets of the Old Testament   101
8. Preaching and Teaching the Laments of the Old Testament   121
9. Preaching and Teaching Old Testament Torah   139
10. Preaching and Teaching Old Testament Praise   153
11. Preaching and Teaching Old Testament Apocalyptic   161

Conclusion: Changing the World with the Word of God   173

Appendix A: Suggested Worksheet for Doing
    Syntactical-Theological Exegesis   179
Appendix B: Biblical Integrity in an Age of
    Theological Pluralism   191
Notes   205
Glossary   213
Subject Index   215
Author Index   217
Scripture Index   219

Introduction

According to some recent polls, the question that laity most want answered about a new pastoral candidate is this: Can he or she preach? This is encouraging, for while the church has made great strides forward based on aspects of the church growth movement and has learned from some of the megachurch groups how to attract the younger generations back into the house of God, the largest challenge that remains is how those same churches can develop a new appetite for the hearing and doing of the Word of God.

Recently I preached at one of the newer megachurches. An enthusiastic crowd of middle teenagers composed the largest block of the congregation in the front center of the auditorium. They responded with rapt attention. It was a joy beyond my ability to describe. Preaching in that kind of situation revitalizes one enormously.

After the service, the pastor asked me to go out and have coffee with him. As we talked, he recounted the obvious blessing of God in the huge numerical increase he had seen as he had applied, not what he had learned in seminary, but what he had gotten from attending seminars offered by those in the megachurch movement. He concluded, "They taught me how to get the kids in. Music is the new language that every one of them understands almost instinctively. But I am afraid that those of us who have experienced such unprecedented growth are headed for a train wreck," he complained.

"Why is that?" I inquired.

"Because we have not been given any help on how we can foster interest and a real appetite for what is needed for spiritual growth and development. Who will help us put theology and biblical teaching into the idiom of the day so that it will capture the eyes, ears, and wills of these new generations?" he pleaded.

His passionate call for help is not unusual. It must not go unheeded.

Fortunately, at the very moment pressure is building for help from a new generation of theologians, scholars, and seminaries, there is evidence that some fresh winds of change have already started to blow. Witness the amazing number of hits on web sites that offer instruction on biblical, theological, and homiletical helps. Note also the new periodicals on preaching and the increasing number of books being published on preaching.

Yet despite this vanguard of favorable signs, there remains a distressing absence of the Old Testament in the church. It is possible to attend some churches for months without ever hearing a sermon from the older testament, which represents well over three-fourths of what our Lord had to say to us. This vacuum is unconscionable for those who claim that the whole Bible is the authoritative Word of God to mankind.

As long ago as 1967, John Bright tried to alleviate some of the alleged roadblocks that believers felt they had in using the Old Testament in his volume, *The Authority of the Old Testament*. At that time, Bright found it best to address the question of *why* we should preach from the older testament rather than tell us *how* we should do it. The time has now come for us to help one another address the question of *how*.

Bright pointed to the theology of the Bible as the key to understanding its message. He asserted that *"no part of the Bible is without authority,* for all parts reflect in one way or another some facet or facets of that structure of faith which is, and must remain, supremely normative for Christian faith and practice."[1]

Bright was even more forceful in laying down a proposition that has raised a firestorm of protest, but one that I will argue is the only way out of our present morass. He declared: "Let us say it clearly: The text has but one meaning, the meaning intended by its author; and there is but one method for discovering that meaning, the grammatical-historical method."[2] This is true, of course. It is the only way to rule out all subjective and personal readings of the text that are without authority or backing of the one who claimed to have received this word as a revelation from God.

Some will immediately object that such a limitation is elusive (for who knows exactly what it is that an author is asserting?) and it also fails to appreciate the enormous complexities that are involved in the act of reading a scriptural text. The assumption is that once a text is produced, it becomes the property of its various readers, who come to that text from a wide assortment of backgrounds and prejudices. Each must have his or her own day in his or her own court to say what each has taken as the meaning for that text. It is this view more than any other that has brought almost all communication on a human level, much less communication from God, to an absolute standstill. Perhaps the best way to demonstrate the folly of this approach is for all of us to get our own meanings of what is being claimed (using their theory of meanings) in their objections. Ultimately, such an approach ends in nonsense.

On the question of where meaning is to be lodged (i.e., in the text, in the community, or in the individual reader), we answer that it is in the text as it is found in the context of the writer's assertions.

All of this will be dealt with more fully in the chapters that follow, but the inroads of postmodernism must not be ignored or taken for granted. It is another strong reason why the teaching and challenging ministry of applying the Old Testament text must not dwindle in our day but remain strong, vigorous, and methodologically sound.

But let us go back to the key that Bright pointed to: theology. Elizabeth Achtemeier countered Bright's appeal to the meaning that the authors of Scripture placed in the text. She claimed, "It must be emphasized that no sermon can become the Word of God for the Christian church if it deals only with the Old Testament apart from the New."[3] In her view every text from the older testament should never stand alone but should always be paired with a text from the New Testament. Fortunately, several scholars challenged her thesis, such as Foster R. McCurley Jr. and Donald Gowan.[4]

But the sad fact is that many in evangelical circles use a method of preaching on the Old Testament that is very similar to this view. The result is that they get very close to, if they do not indeed practice, what we know as eisegesis, that is, "read-ing [meaning] into" the text. The result is a flat Bible in which ideas found elsewhere in Scripture are equal to similar ideas found in all parts of the Bible in part and in the whole. It is not that such preachers act as if they do not possess the full canon of Scripture or as if God were not the author of it in its entirety, but it is rather that their methodology is flawed. We first must establish what the text of the Old Testament is asserting, and only then should we draw in additional information on that sub-ject, which God has seen fit to give us in the later progress of revelation.

Much more helpful in getting at the meaning of these Old Tes-tament texts is the recent development of first observing the par-ticular genre in which a text was cast as the most basic clue on how to interpret it and how to preach on that text. Donald Gowan said it best: "That ancient writer used the genre which was best suited to convey the particular message which burdened him, and the question is, can that help the preacher who wants to speak to contemporaries as effectively and persuasively as pos-sible?"[5] This, then, is what we aspire to do in this volume after we have treated the preliminary matters that have already been mentioned as roadblocks. May our Lord grant to all of us wis-dom and a passionate desire to communicate with all of our heart and soul the fabulous message of the gospel at this criti-cal moment in history.

This book began as a set of lectures first delivered on June 2–14, 2000. I am grateful to Dr. Joseph Shoa, president of the Biblical Seminary of the Philippines, for his kind invitation to teach forty-four enthusiastic seminarians. Their critiques and encouragements were most helpful in formulating the chapters now before you.

I must also express gratitude to my research assistant, Jason McKnight, for his help in locating some difficult bibliographic sources and to my editor at Baker Academic, Brian Bolger. Spe-cial thanks to Rev. Dr. Dorington Little for permission to include his sermon on the lament of Psalm 77. Their assistance is deeply appreciated. The responsibility for the resulting product is my own and one for which I must be faulted, not them. May God be pleased to use this book for his honor and glory.

Part 1

The Need to Preach and Teach from the Old Testament

1

The Value of the Old Testament for Today

Quite often when I have the opportunity to speak or preach at a church or Christian institution, I am asked: "You are not going to speak from the Old Testament, are you?" Obviously the expected answer is that no one who is thinking correctly, or even as a Christian, would venture to do such a bizarre thing as address contemporary issues and the needs of our day by going back to something as antique and remote as the Old Testament.

But that is indeed what I have done time and again, for I have been impressed with how relevant and powerful a message that portion of the biblical text shares with the New Testament. The time has come for a whole new evaluation of our reasons for avoiding this section of the Bible. Along with the argument for turning to the Old Testament for answers to contemporary issues must also come some practical helps on how this task can be carried out without doing an injustice either to the older text or to the needs of the waiting church.

The Old Testament needs about as much defending as a lion! Yet it clearly is overlooked and frequently neglected in the preaching and teaching ministry of the church. This neglect is all the more baffling when its claims and right to be received as the powerful Word of God are just as strong as those of the New Testament. Therefore, it is incumbent that we hear the Old Testament's own case for itself once again. This case can be set forth in four major theses.

It Is the Powerful Word of God

The earlier testament is light years away from being a mere word *from* mortals written *to* humanity *about* themselves! Instead, it presents itself as possessing divine authority with a sufficiency that transcends what mere mortals can create or expound for their contemporaries or for later generations.

True, God employed the distinctive personalities, literary skills, vocabulary, and unique ways each writer had of expressing himself, as anyone who has read the Bible in the original languages has noticed. But God's revelation was not thereby hampered or distorted like a sunbeam that is refracted when it passes through a stained glass window. If this analogy must be used, then let it be noted that the architect that built the sun, from which the sunbeam originated, is the same architect who built the stained glass window, which in this case would be analogous to the writers of the Old Testament. God prepared both the writers, with all the uniqueness and particularity that each brings to the task of writing Scripture, and the revelation itself.

The point is this: the preparation of the authors was just as significant a work of God as was the revelation that came from God. Thus, each writer was given experiences, cultural settings, a range of vocabulary, and special idiosyncrasies so that they would express themselves in styles absolutely their own but with the end result being precisely what God wanted for each section of his revelation.

This preparation of the writer began as early as the day he was born. The prophet Jeremiah knew he was called while he was still in his mother's womb (Jer. 1:4–5), while Isaiah's call to minister on behalf of God's word came out of his sense of need, apparently later in life (Isa. 1–5). If Jeremiah illustrates what an internal call of God is like, then Isaiah shows us what God's external call is like.

How, then, can each writer be so uniquely himself and yet so true to the disclosure God wanted to get across to humanity? Must we sacrifice either human originality or divine authority? We cannot have it both ways—or can we?

It is evident to any student beginning to read in the original languages of the Old Testament (Hebrew and Aramaic) that there are very clear differences in the levels of difficulty, grammar, vocabulary, and styles in the thirty-nine books of the Old Testament. This certainly makes the case for the individuality of each of the writers. But instead of this being a mere word of mortals, the repeated claim of the writers themselves is that what they wrote was a disclosure from God that was to be distinguished from their own words. For example, Jeremiah 23:28–29 enjoined:

> "Let the prophet who has a dream tell his dream, but let the one who has my word speak it faithfully. For what has straw to do with grain," declares the LORD. "Is not my word like fire," declares the LORD, "and like a hammer that breaks a rock in pieces?"

To confuse the prophet's own words and dreams with God's word and vision was as silly as confusing straw and chaff with real grain on that straw stem!

The apostle Paul would have no part in a diminution of the Old Testament, for he instructed his youthful friend Timothy in 2 Timothy 3:16 that,

> All Scripture is God-breathed and is useful for
>   teaching,
>   rebuking,
>   correcting
>   and training in righteousness.

One must recall that the "Scripture" (Greek: *graphe*, "writing") that was available to Timothy when Paul wrote was the Old Testament. All of it, the whole of the Old Testament, was "God-breathed." It came as a product of God. Therefore, if we are to have a balanced and full presentation of all of God's truth, it is absolutely essential that we include the Old Testament in our teaching and preaching.

Moreover, the Old Testament is useful for it has at least four functions: (1) teaching, (2) rebuking, (3) correcting, and (4) training us in righteousness. To this Paul also adds in 2 Timothy 3:15 that the Old Testament is "able to make [us] wise for salvation through faith in Christ Jesus." Few think that such a good result as one's own personal salvation through faith in Jesus Christ could come from teaching and preaching from the Old Testament, but the apostle Paul taught that it could—and he taught that under the inspiration of the sovereign Lord.[1]

Our day is not the only time when the Word of God has been scarce, hard to find, out of vogue, or seemingly lacking in power or effectiveness in those cases where it is exposed to the people. One could cite a similar situation when young Samuel was growing up in the sanctuary under the tutelage of the priest Eli. Accordingly, the story began on the note that "in those days the word of the LORD was rare; there were not many visions" (1 Sam. 3:1). Without the light of revelation, the whole fabric of society was put at risk. That point was also made in the Book of Proverbs, which warned, "Where there is no revelation [Hebrew: ḥazôn, "vision" or "disclosure" from God], the people perish" (Prov. 29:18, my translation). The Hebrew term used for "perish" is the same one that appears in the golden calf episode in Exodus 32:25, where the people "cast off all restraint" and "ran wild" in acts of sacred prostitution in front of the calf they had just created. That was exactly what was happening in the days of young Samuel, for the high priest's sons were imitating the same reckless path of destroying themselves even while they presided as priests at the altar of God. Meanwhile, the word of God remained scarce and was rarely announced or taught to the people.

Possession of a word from God was no small favor or treasure, for it continues to be second in importance only to the gift of God's Son. But mere *possession* of that word alone will not be enough to fortify the community in times of need. In fact, continual neglect of that word can lead to God himself making that word scarce so that few can find it and thus profit from applying its message. In that case, mortals cannot manufacture it, duplicate it, or replace it with an alleged alternative.

Such a scarcity of God's word would be a sign of God's judgment on his people and their leaders who had helped to create this barrenness. It would represent a setting similar to those horrible words found in Amos 8:11–12:

> "The days are coming," declares the Sovereign LORD, "when I will send a famine through the land—not a famine of food or a thirst for water, but a famine of hearing the words of the LORD. Men

will stagger from sea to sea and wander from north to east, searching for the word of the LORD, but they will not find it."

Sometimes God gives us what we want (when we refuse to hear his word), but he also sends a leanness to our souls as a result (Ps. 106:15). In these instances, God grows silent and the darkness of our day thickens as an unbearable sadness and gloom sets in over us.

The only known cure for this is the cry that was heard in the Reformation: *post tenebras lux,* "After darkness, light!" That is why Calvin and his successors reasoned that the only way *light* was going to come to God's people and to the city of Geneva, Switzerland, would be through the preaching of the Scriptures. Hence, six sermons a week were prescribed according to the Ordinances of the Church of Geneva in A.D. 1541. There was to be a sermon at dawn on Sunday, and another at the usual hour of 9 A.M. Catechism for the children was to take place at noon, followed by a sermon at 3 P.M. and three more sermons on Monday, Wednesday, and Friday. Only in this manner would light return and the darkness be invaded, they reasoned. Should we not follow these Genevans in establishing, as they did, something more than the twenty-five-minute homily or one ten- to fifteen-minute topical sermon given each Sunday morning as the total source for our Christian maturation for the whole week? And should not a portion of that expanded repertoire of biblical texts include a distinctive preaching and teaching mission from Old Testament texts?

That word from God can startle us just as it shocked the priest Eli (1 Sam. 3:2–14). It was startling in its call, for repeatedly God called to the young boy Samuel (vv. 2–10). The words "call" or "called" appear no less than eleven times in verses 4–10 of 1 Samuel 3. Nevertheless, God does not rebuke Samuel for being dim-witted or slow to respond; he merely "came and stood there, calling as at the other times" (v. 10). The patience and tenderness of our Lord is in itself amazing.

But just as amazing and startling is the content of that word. In this case it was the word that the Lord had Samuel deliver to Eli. The sovereign God was "about to do something in Israel that [would] make the ears of everyone who hear[d] of it tingle" (v. 11). Because Eli failed to restrain his sons, God would judge his family and the guilt of their household would never be atoned for by sacrifice or offering (vv. 12–14). Hence, the word of God would involve a blessed call on one man for service to God but a visitation of judgment on another for failure to act in accordance with the published Word.

In so doing God demonstrated that he was sovereign over all (1 Sam. 3:15–18). He was sovereign over the speaker (vv. 15–17) and sovereign over the audience (v. 18). Thus we are taught in Scripture to say "Amen," not only to the blessings of God, but also to the judgments of God.

The story of Samuel ends with the word of God accrediting his servant Samuel (1 Sam. 3:19–4:1a). As a matter of fact, God "let none of his words fall to the ground" (v. 19). Herein lay the validation, confirmation, and security of Samuel's proclamation of the divine revelation. And that is what will validate the preaching of the Old Testament in our day as well: the sovereign validation of the Lord himself.[2]

It Leads Us to Jesus the Messiah

One of the tragic results of separating the Old Testament from the New is that the believing community fails to see that Jesus' life, ministry, death, and resurrection were clearly anticipated long before the events occurred. By viewing the older testament as a message that is non-Christian, the expectation is set in advance for some that there is nothing Christological or messianic to be gained from studying, much less reading, teaching, and preaching, the Old Testament. But such a view flies in the face of the evidence from the text itself.

The Messiah is at the heart of the message of that neglected portion of the Bible. For example, according to rabbinical calculations, there are some 456 Old Testament texts that refer either directly to the Messiah or to the messianic times.[3] Even though this number is inflated by the particular standards of scholarship used in some communities, what remains when the list is reduced is still extremely impressive.[4]

Sadly, a significant portion of modern scholarship shares a skeptical attitude toward the messianic consciousness of the Old

Testament writers. Typical of such judgments is the conclusion of Joachim Becker: "There is no evidence for true messianism until the second century B.C."[5] Becker would have us believe that it was only on the threshold of the New Testament that we begin to see any evidence for a Messiah! The amazing thing is that Becker himself realized that such a conclusion would run counter to some pretty strong evidence from those early believers in the first Christian century who were still without a New Testament in any of its sections or parts. He allowed: "Such a conclusion [that he had just made above] would contradict one of the most central concerns of the New Testament, which insists with unprecedented frequency, intensity, and unanimity that Christ was proclaimed in advance in the Old Testament. Historical-critical scholarship can never set aside this assertion of the New Testament."[6] Becker will go to even greater lengths in destroying his own conclusions. He wrote, "To find Christ at every step on our way through the history of Israel and the Old Testament is not only no deception but also a duty imposed on us by the inspired testimony of the New Testament, the meaning of which we must strive to understand."[7]

Indeed, there is an organic system of messianic prophecy that can be found in the Old Testament, which is in full accord with the fulfillments of the New Testament. All too few have noticed the organic unity of the total argument, often settling for much less by picking up a verse here or there in an abstract and random manner.

The interpreter need not resort to settling for a double set of meanings in order to squeeze out of the Old Testament some messianic possibilities. On the contrary, one must be able to show that the Old Testament writers were aware of a very decided nexus between the temporal/historical events in many of their prophecies and their climactic fulfillment in the Messiah—and this can be done legitimately without doing violence to the ordinary rules of interpretation.

Those who argue that the messianic meaning, that which points to Jesus as the Messiah, remains hidden in the text oppose the apostles, who boldly announced that the events that occurred during the days of Jesus happened exactly as the Old Testament had predicted! The Old Testament cannot have a more obvious meaning along with a hidden Christian meaning. Had that been the case, quoting the verses for nonbelievers and trying to convince them that Jesus had been fully anticipated in the Old Testament predictions would have amounted to foolishness. If we incorrectly argue that this meaning had been hidden in the earlier revelation of God, how then could it be persuasive for those considering whether Jesus was the one sent from God according to his plans from all eternity?

James H. Charlesworth has argued that "the term 'Messiah' in the Old Testament does not denote God's final agent in the history of salvation. . . . The New Testament concept of 'The Messiah' is linked with the Old Testament through the theology of Early Judaism."[8]

But this is to miss the repeated claim of the Old Testament text itself. The term *Messiah* is indeed used only nine times of the coming Anointed One who was to arrive in the person of Jesus Christ.[9] Yet both the Jewish community (especially in pre-Christian days) and the early church found scores, if not hundreds, of texts supporting a messianic interpretation as we have already shown in the preceding argument.

As early as the day of Pentecost (Acts 2:16–36), the apostle Peter used the Old Testament to demonstrate that Jesus' death, burial, and resurrection had been clearly anticipated by the writers of the Old Testament. Peter appealed to the prophet Joel (Joel 2:28–31), to the psalmist (Ps. 16), and to King David's understanding (2 Sam. 7; Ps. 110) to make these same points prior to the appearance of any New Testament literature. A few days later, as Peter and John were going into the temple, he healed a lame man at the temple gate (Acts 3). This occasioned another sermon from Peter, in which he again made direct references to Abraham, Isaac, and Jacob, noting how they pointed to "what [God] had foretold through all the prophets" (Acts 3:18), namely, that Christ must suffer. Peter asserted that Christ was "that prophet" about whom Moses had written. Moses had expected God to raise up such a one to appear in these days. This pattern of appealing to the Old Testament to demonstrate that Christ is the Messiah was repeated in Stephen's speech in Acts 7 and in Paul's speech in the synagogue at Antioch (Acts 13). It is not a case of the early disciples borrowing from Judaism, the newly formed Jewish religion that began in the Babylonian exile in which the temple would now be replaced by the synagogue, the priest would be replaced by the scribe or wise man, and the sacrifices would be replaced by prayers. The apostles' appeal was directly and solely to the earlier and prior text of the Old Testament itself.

Jesus' own testimony to himself was no less clear: "These [Old Testament texts] are the Scriptures that testify about me" (John 5:39b). Moreover, in Jesus' own hour of temptation, when faced by Satan himself, his response to each of the three temptations was to cite the Old Testament as his definite and authoritative remonstrance. Jesus had no need to accommodate either his Jewish listeners or the devil, as some allege. On the contrary, it was a conviction shared by both the Lord and the evil one: the Scriptures were the authoritative Word of God. On that point the devil could not be faulted!

It Deals with the Questions of Life

The scope of the Old Testament's teaching on the great questions of life is extremely broad and startling in its practicality. It covers everything from questions of human dignity and treatment of the environment in the opening chapters of Genesis to the nature and purpose of marital love in the Song of Solomon and a theology of culture in the Book of Ecclesiastes.

Its moral laws address such values and sanctities as the absolute uniqueness of God, the worth and dignity of mortals, and respect for human life, for parents, for marriage, for property, and for truth. The civil laws, on the other hand, illustrate issues like public safety, treatment of orphans, property rights, and respect for authority. No less helpful are the ceremonial laws, which teach us to draw a line in the sand, demarcating the sacred and the secular and setting apart that which is holy from that which is common and ordinary.

If the Book of Lamentations is needed to develop a theology of suffering, then the Psalms are needed just as much to teach us how to praise and worship God.

Both the earlier prophets (Joshua, Judges, Samuel, and Kings) and the latter prophets (Isaiah, Jeremiah, Ezekiel, and the twelve Minor Prophets, according to the arrangement in the Hebrew

Bible) unfold the promise-plan of God. They also give us practical lessons we can use as we observe both the failures and the successes of earlier individuals and nations. The point is clear: those who refuse to learn from history are doomed, as the saying goes, to repeat its mistakes.

It Was Used as the Exclusive Authority in the Early Church

Even though we have already made reference to this fact, it bears a distinctive emphasis of its own. The fact is that whenever the word "Scripture(s)" (*graphe, graphai*) appears in the New Testament, it almost always points to the Old Testament, whether in its Greek translation, known as the Septuagint, or in its Hebrew and Aramaic text. It was to these texts that the Christians went, as did the Bereans, for example, to find how Jesus had been anticipated in the plan and purpose of God in that earlier testament.

Not every Jew or every early follower of Jesus caught on. One need only remember those two disciples who were walking on that first Easter Sunday to the village of Emmaus when Jesus joined them (Luke 24). Cleopas and that other disciple were so overtaken by their sadness that they failed to notice that the one who accompanied them was Jesus himself.

Their failure went deeper than that, however. They had no idea that the events they were now experiencing had been foretold long ago in the very Scriptures that they held to be the Word of God. This intellectual faux pas calls down Jesus' stern rebuke: "How foolish you are, and how slow of heart to believe all that the prophets have spoken! Did not the Christ have to suffer these things and then enter his glory?" (Luke 24:25–26). In the next verse Jesus went on, "And beginning with Moses and all the Prophets, he explained to them what was said in all the Scriptures concerning himself."

Nowhere in the New Testament can one find evidence advocating that the writers went outside the boundaries of the Old Testament text to gain their view of the Messiah, or that they just rejected outright what these texts taught about the coming one. The "story" the early church told was the story of the promise-plan of God and the line of the "seed" that would end in David's final son, Jesus. This was the gospel they proclaimed.

Our English word *gospel* goes back to the Middle English *godspel*, which meant the "good story" and by a change of inflection, the "God-story."[10] Thus, the gospel was the story of that series of interconnected events written to inform us about the person and work of the Messiah.

But there is more to be said about the early Christians' appeal to the Old Testament, for it was more than a mere series of prooftexts for the identity and mission of the Messiah. In Romans 9–11, Paul grapples with the issue of whether God has been faithful to his promises made to Israel. He is interested not only in the promise concerning the "seed," but also in the "land," *eretz Israel*, and the blessings that were to come to all nations of the earth through Israel's man of promise.

Paul could hardly contain himself as he traced the concepts of Israel's adoption as sons, the divine glory that was theirs, the covenants, the receiving of the law, the temple worship, and the promises (Rom. 9:4). Yet he was troubled enough to ask the key question: Had God failed to do what he had promised? Such an idea was anathema to Paul, "for God's gifts and his call [were] irrevocable" (Rom. 11:29). Even though the nation Israel had for the moment been cut out of its own tree (which was rooted in the promises made to the patriarchs), this exclusion would only last until the times of the Gentiles were fulfilled and the full number of the Gentiles had come into the body of believers (Rom. 11:25). But then there would be a grafting of Israel back into the tree they were cut out of, as they returned in those latter days in great numbers to full belief in their Messiah. Paul was exuberant. Such knowledge astounded him:

> O the depth of the riches and wisdom and knowledge of God!
> How unsearchable are [God's] judgments and how inscrutable
> [God's] ways. (Rom. 11:33 NRSV)

God could not and would not go back on all that he had promised in the Old Testament. No wonder the early church found both a ready apologetic for the Messiah's claims and such great comfort in the Old Testament.

Conclusion

The Old Testament was the Bible of the early church. Yet one more objection can be heard from some detractors. "Now that we have the New Testament, should we not go to the New Testament *first* to form an understanding of the Bible's teachings and then go *backward* into the Old Testament, interpreting it in the light of the New Testament?" This approach is advocated so frequently in the church today that it must be faced squarely.[11]

This whole approach is wrongheaded historically, logically, and biblically. As we have seen, the first New Testament believers tested what they had heard from Jesus and his disciples against what was written in the Old Testament. They had no other canon or source of help. How, then, were they able to get it right?

Thus, from a methodological point of view, reading the Bible backward is incorrect historically as well as procedurally. What is more, the early church knew the Old Testament to be true; therefore, logically, they could not have tested what was established (and true) for them (possessing only the Old Testament) by what was being received as new (the New Testament)! That would be a reversal of the natural, historical, and logical order of things.

Finally, Israel had been taught biblically in passages like Deuteronomy 13 and 18 to test new teachings or claims to divine authority by what God had already revealed in his Word (i.e., in the Old Testament). Therefore, preaching and teaching the Bible in a backward methodology can produce a message that is also methodologically backward!

In validating claims to authenticity, we move from what is already acknowledged to be true to that which builds on it. What, then, is the case for interpreting the Bible in a forward, rather than a backward, approach?[12]

1. To reject the Old Testament as the *prior*, authoritative revelation of God is to reject the Bible's own basis for determining who is and who is not the Messiah. Jesus located the failure of the Jewish audiences in their failure to believe what Moses wrote. In John 5:46–47 Jesus declared, "If you

believed Moses, you would believe Me; for he wrote of Me. But if you do not believe his writings, how will you believe My words?" (NASB). Exactly so! Dismissing the Old Testament and reducing the scope of your study only to the New Testament will logically raise this question: "How can I believe what God has said *en toto* in the New Testament if I tend to not believe or trust what he has said in the Old?"

2. The New Testament Scriptures base their claim to being authoritative on the Old Testament. That is why Matthew 1 begins with a genealogy that stretches from Genesis to the New Testament.

3. The foundation of Jesus' teaching was the Old Testament. If any new teaching contradicted the *Tenach* (Jewish acronym for the Old Testament), it had to be rejected, for Deuteronomy 12:32 warned: "See that you do all I command you; do not add to it or take away from it."

4. Paul also based his teaching on the Old Testament. He preached what he had received from the Old Testament Scriptures. Said he, "For what I received I passed on to you as of first importance: that Christ died for our sins *according to the Scriptures,* that he was buried, that he was raised on the third day *according to the Scriptures*" (1 Cor. 15:3–4, italics added). But even more definitively, when Paul was on trial for his life, he affirmed, "Now I am standing trial for the hope of the promise made by God to our fathers" (Acts 26:6 NASB). He concluded by saying, "And so, having obtained help from God, I stand to this day . . . stating nothing but what the Prophets and Moses said was going to take place" (Acts 26:22 NASB). His testimony was that he believed "everything that [was] in accordance with the Law, and that [was] written in the Prophets" (Acts 24:14 NASB). Even under arrest in Rome, Paul called the Jewish community together to explain what his message was. He saw himself as "testifying to the kingdom of God and trying to persuade them concerning Jesus both from the law of Moses and from the prophets from morning to evening" (Acts 28:23, my translation).

The Old Testament can stand on its own, for it has done so both in the pre-Christian and the early Christian centuries. To make the preaching or teaching of the Old Testament contingent on a prior commitment to making normative for all matters of faith the teaching at the end of God's revelation (i.e., the New Testament) obscures the uniqueness of many of the Old Testament's teachings. It also trivializes up to three-fourths of what God had to say to us. The tendency to interpret the Bible backward is a serious procedural problem, for it will leave a large vacuum in our teachings and provide seedbeds for tomorrow's heresies. It is reductionistic to level out the Bible to say only what the New Testament has said!

The value of the Old Testament is immeasurable for all believers. To avoid it is to miss approximately three-fourths of what our Lord has to say to us today, whether we will hear it or not!

2

The Problem of the Old Testament for Today

Instead of receiving the Old Testament with gratitude as a gift from God, all too many in Christ's church view it as an albatross around the necks of contemporary Christians. They struggle with questions like these: What is the significance of the Old Testament for us today? Why should believers even bother with the Old Testament now that we have the New Testament? Aren't there a lot of problems in using a book like the Old Testament, especially when so much of it is no longer in force and normative for the church? Questions such as these ultimately raise the issue of the Old Testament as a major problem, if not the master problem of theology.

Is the Old Testament the Master Problem of Theology?

In 1955 Emil Kraeling warned, "The Old Testament problem . . . is not just one of many. It is the master problem of theology."[1] This is an accurate assessment of the situation, in my judgment, for as soon as one makes an incorrect judgment with regard to the Old Testament, the trickle-down effects ripple all the way through the rest of one's theology. For example, once one concludes, as some have, that Abraham's belief in God in Genesis 15:6 means that he merely became a theist, in the sense that he decided there must be a God and he would put his trust in him, the results of that interpretation begin showing up in one's Christology and missiology. That false conclusion has led many to conclude that it is not necessary for one's faith to be grounded in Jesus, for one can experience saving faith by merely believing that there must be a God out there, just as Abraham allegedly did. Christians know that Acts 4:12 says that there is no name other than the name of Jesus by which we can be saved, but once again some incorrectly assume that the rules differ between the testaments. But it would introduce a grave problem in Old Testament exegesis if we held that Abraham merely believed in God. To say Abraham believed in God, without making reference to the promise of the seed that was to come, would mean that now a weak theology was mastering our concepts of salvation, missions, and the necessity of belief in Jesus.

A. H. J. Gunneweg echoed the same sentiment that the Old Testament was a master problem of theology when he concluded:

> It would be no exaggeration to understand the hermeneutical problem of the Old Testament as *the* problem of Christian theology. It is not just one problem among others. It is *the* problem because all other questions of theology are affected in one way or another by the solution to this problem.[2]

One need only review the great christological and trinitarian debates in the church, not to mention those relating to the atonement and the doctrine of salvation, to validate the fact that the Old Testament is indeed *the* master problem of theology.[3] A misstep in this testament often means a misstep down the line in theology and practice of the faith.

Does the Old Testament Have a Center or a *Mitte?*

Just as the writers of the Old Testament did not write in a vacuum, neither did the original readers or the early church read the ancient Scriptures in a vacuum. They read the books and authors of the Old Testament, instead, out of a sense of wholeness and a connectedness with one another. The text was treated

as an ongoing story of the plan and purpose of God played out
on the historical canvas of those times in which its participants
were located.

The case for the unity of the testament can be traced in the
way that later writers quote and make allusions to previous
events, persons, and words, a method that could be used as a
precedent in our own day. But this is contrary to the main mood
in contemporary biblical scholarship. The charge against the
unity and connectedness of the text is that the materials of the
Old Testament are just too diverse, disparate, and variegated to
allow for any central motif or organizing plan. But to draw this
conclusion is to give up on the fact that there was an organizing divine mind behind the whole testament. Instead, all too
often God is deleted from the picture and a multiplicity of minds,
wills, and purposes are put in place of God's own mind, purpose, and plan.

If there is a key that unlocks this quest for an organizing center, what is it? I contend that it is to be found in the *promise-
plan* of God. No text substantiates this claim better than does
1 Peter 1:3–12. As Peter discussed "so great a salvation" that
Christian believers have, he concluded it was this same salvation that the prophets had looked into as well. These prophets
had "enquired and searched diligently" (v. 10 KJV) concerning
this salvation.

"But isn't that precisely the point of the objection to any kind
of unified or holistic plan or center to the Old Testament?" some
will protest. After all, if the prophets were scratching their heads
about this salvation, how could they have been knowledgeable
on this same subject? Were they perplexed, or were they precise
in what they wrote and taught?

The answer is that it was only the issues of the *timing* and the
circumstances connected with Messiah and his works that baf-
fled them in 1 Peter 1:10–12. On the main facts, however, they
were crystal clear: (1) they knew they were speaking about Messiah, (2) they knew Messiah must suffer, (3) they knew Messiah
would also be glorified and triumph, (4) they knew the order,
that is, that the suffering would come first and then the glory,
and finally, (5) they knew they were writing not just for their
own times but for "us" in the Christian church as well. That is

what Peter taught the young church to whom he wrote his epistle in the Christian era.

Accordingly, I believe that the writers of the Old Testament were aware of what they were saying. They saw some unity and a connective link to the successive books. While a unifying structure is extremely important, it should not be seen as a grid placed over the Bible or one that was imposed *from the outside*. It must be a structure and plan that springs from *within* the successive Old Testament texts themselves.

Does the Old Testament Exhibit Such a Unity?

Scholars have suggested all sorts of central themes for the Old Testament, such as the holiness of God, communion with God, the rule of God, the kingdom of God, and the covenant. Each idea has its merits, but each fails to show from *within* the Old Testament itself that it was the divinely intended organizing center for the entire Old Testament.

If I were to choose a text of the Old Testament that most succinctly states the divine mind and brings together all the multiplicity of themes, I would choose Genesis 12:3. It reads: "In your seed all the nations of the earth shall be blessed" (my translation). There is the organizing plan of the whole Bible.[4]

Albrektson wrote in his *History and the Gods*, "If I could accept Genesis 12:3 as being passive in form (in the Hebrew form of the verb), I would see this as the whole plan of God."[5] But the verb is indeed passive[6] in form in the Hebrew, and that is the way it was quoted in the intertestamental period as well as in the New Testament. Thus, the plan of God can be defined as a word or declaration from God that he would form a nation and out of that nation he would bring the one through whom salvation would come to all the nations. This theme can be referred to as the "promise-plan of God."

It was not until New Testament times that those writers chose to designate this plan by the single word *promise*. It is so used in all but six New Testament books (i.e., with the exception of Matthew, Mark, John, James, Jude, and Revelation). The noun "promise" is used fifty-one times and the verb "to promise" eleven times in the New Testament. In almost every one of these instances, it was used to refer to God's ongoing plan and his declaration announced repeatedly in the Old Testament. However, in the Old Testament no single term dominates as a designation for this plan of God. Instead, the Old Testament used a constellation of terms, such as God's "oath," his "word," his "kingdom," his "house," and the like. This promise-plan of God grew throughout the Old Testament as it took on more and more items within the single plan of God. It included missions, inheritance of land, the fear of God, how to live wisely, and how to use one's leisure time as a gift from God. It even embraced marital love and marriage relationships.

Paul made the same summary in his Antioch of Pisidia speech: "We preach to you the good news of the *promise* made to the fathers, that God has fulfilled this *promise* to our children in that He raised up Jesus from the dead" (Acts 13:32–33 NASB, italics added). Even more significantly, Paul summarized his whole life's work before King Agrippa in Acts 26:6–7, saying, "And now I stand here because of my hope in the *promise*." I am on trial, Paul continued, for "hope in the *promise* made by God to our fathers to which our twelve tribes hope to attain" [ESV].

If we take all sixty-two New Testament references in the twenty-one books that mention "promise," they break down as follows: 20 percent of the promise references are to the nation of Israel, 16 percent deal with the promise of the resurrection from the dead, 11 percent concern the promise of Jesus as Messiah, 6 percent deal with Christ's second coming, 20 percent refer to the promise of redemption from sin, 16 percent concern the promise of the gospel for the nations, and another 5 percent relate to the Gentiles as such.

The four most unique moments in the promise-plan of God, acting like four great mountain peaks in the Old Testament range, are: Genesis 3:15, Genesis 12:2–3, 2 Samuel 7, and Jeremiah 31:31–34. These are, respectively, the one promise-plan made to Eve, to Abraham, and to David, and the new covenant made with Israel.

Grasping some sense of the wholeness of God's plan will make it much easier to teach and preach the individual parts of this totality in the Old Testament. Or, to put it another way, it is difficult to do expository preaching and teaching without a biblical theology that arises naturally from the text of Scripture itself. One must have some idea of what the forest is like before attempting to exegete the individual trees, branches, or leaves. Biblical theology becomes a most important component in the preacher's and teacher's understanding as he or she approaches the text.

Does the Old Testament Exemplify Legalism or Grace?

All too frequently believers think that the term "Old Testament" is synonymous with the law of Moses, a law that has passed away now that the New Testament has come. If that is true, then why bother with the Old Testament? Some quote Martin Luther to establish this latter complaint. Said Luther, "Christ abolished all the laws of Moses that ever were."[7]

Had Luther been correct, there would be no laws against murder, theft, idolatry, adultery, bearing false witness, dishonoring one's parents, and more. Luther's statement, as it stands, is in need of major corrections.

Irenaeus, a disciple of Polycarp, who in turn was the disciple of the apostle John, wrote in A.D. 180 just the opposite of what Luther would later be understood to advocate:

> And the apostles who were with James allowed the Gentiles to act freely, yielding us up to the Spirit of God [Acts 15]. But they themselves, while knowing the same God, continued in the ancient observances. . . . Thus did the Apostles, whom the Lord made witnesses of every action and of every doctrine . . . scrupulously act according to the dispensation of the Mosaic law.[8]

The law itself was never given as a means of salvation or redemption. Instead, it was set forth, beginning in Exodus 20 (the Decalogue), in the context of redemption: "I am the LORD your God, who brought you out of Egypt, out of the land of slavery."

What, then, could have been the law's purpose? It was the means by which we came to know what sin is (Rom. 7:7) and that sin is prohibited (Rom. 4:15). Sin was in the world before the law came (Rom. 5:13), but when the law came, it not only forbade sin, but also showed us what is right and how we ought now to live.

Of course the law promised death to all who broke it, but the law was given out of God's love, mercy, and grace. Here was God's standard of holiness and the measure for deciding who and what was "in-the-right," or "righteous."

Jesus warned in Matthew 5:17, "Don't even think [apparently, he knew some would be tempted to do so] that I came to destroy the law and the prophets. I have not come to abolish them, but to bring them to fullness," that is, to fulfill them (my translation). In fact, so serious is this matter that Jesus warns in Matthew 5:19, "Anyone who breaks one of the least of these commandments and teaches others to do the same will be called least in the kingdom of heaven."

But some still protest, "Didn't Paul teach that the law was abolished?"

He did not! Listen to him ask this question: "Do we, then, nullify the law by this faith? Not at all! Rather, we uphold [establish] the law" (Rom. 3:31).

Not to be outdone, our objector still complains, "Did not the new covenant, though, replace the old covenant of the law in Jeremiah 31:31–34?" On the contrary, the new covenant retained the *same law*, God's law given to Moses, with the additional promise that God would write it on our hearts instead of writing it on stone. Even though there are differences in the law due to its built-in obsolescence or its only being applicable to some people in distinct circumstances,[9] God's law is still at the center of the new covenant.

But some still persist in claiming that grace is not present in the Old Testament. However, anyone who has noted the long-suffering patience of God and his steadfast refusal to rescind his promise to Israel cannot be serious in making such a protest against the Old Testament. To take only one example, note how in the midst of reciting a litany of Israel's transgressions during the days of the Judges, God affirms, "I will never break my covenant with you" (Judg. 2:1). What is this but a demonstration of grace itself!

Is the Old Testament to Be Made Over into the New Testament?

If we should not advocate abolishing or rejecting the Old Testament, must we *Christianize* it, some ask, in order to preserve its usefulness for the church? But this idea too we must reject. What, then, does the Old Testament have to do with the New? Are there no dissimilarities or differences between the two testaments?

The church must not be faulted entirely for being so confused over this question, for it has been taught at least six different answers concerning the question of the continuity or discontinuity found between the testaments.

The Old Testament Is to Be Expunged

The first answer is an extreme one. It declares that the earlier testament was a waste and itself a pagan religion. This is what Marcion, Schleiermacher, Harnack, and the younger Delitzsch taught. Marcion, a wealthy merchant born in Pontus, on the Black Sea, split from the early church in A.D. 144, forming his own sect because of this issue. However, his views on these matters were condemned by the Edict of Constantine in the fourth century. Marcion taught that the Old Testament God was a demigod, who was harsh and cruel. The whole Old Testament, along with the Old Testament allusions or quotations in the New Testament, had to be expunged from the holy book of the church. Friedrich Schleiermacher, Adolph Harnack, and Friedrick Delitzsch all came to very similar conclusions.

The Old Testament Is a Negative Lesson

A second solution is to use the Old Testament as a negative lesson and a history of failure. Its messages are best summarized as a lesson in what we ought not to do, much as many incorrectly read the twelve chapters of Ecclesiastes as a natural person's point of view with the only helpful point coming in the final two verses of the book. But, again, must we not be more inspired than the text we are examining in order to determine what will and what will not pass as the message of God? By what criteria will we separate what must be taken positively, if anything, from that which is negative?

The Old Testament Provides Only Background Material for the New Testament

Once again, the Old Testament has no particular word for the church or subsequent generations. According to this theory, it was merely preparatory for the real word of God (!) that was later to come in the New Testament. Accordingly, the first testament is like a preface to a book that tells us that good things are going to come in the chapters that follow.

The Old Testament Is Merely a Providential Preparation for Christ

Another attempt at solving the problem of continuity and discontinuity between the testaments is one that assigns to the first testament only a providential role in preparation for the second. While the words and events that are recorded in the Old Testament are not directed to the church or anyone else in later times, these same words and events did prepare the ground for Christ's coming and his real revelation that came in the message of the New Testament.

The Old Testament Preserves Types or Allegories That Illustrate Christian Truth

Here, too, the norm is the New Testament, which, when read back into the Old Testament, seems to uncover concealed messages that were encoded in types or allegories. These can be used illustratively but not in a didactic or straightforward way.

The Old Testament Is Part of the Unified Plan of God for All Times and All Peoples

My solution is to understand the two testaments as part of one continuing, unified plan of God. Paul summarized this concept when he argued in Romans 15:8–9, "For I tell you that Christ has become a servant of the Jews on behalf of God's truth, to confirm the promises made to the patriarchs so that the Gentiles may glorify God for his mercy." This harks back to Genesis 12:3, for Christ became a servant to the Jewish people for one great purpose: so that he could confirm the promise-plan given to Abraham, Isaac, and Jacob, that in Abram's seed, "all the families of the earth will be blessed" (NASB). The proof of that thesis, as indicated by Paul in Romans 15:9–12, is to be found in the following Old Testament texts: 2 Samuel 22:50; Psalm 18:49; Deuteronomy 32:43; Psalm 117:1; and Isaiah 11:10.

"Has nothing at all changed between the two testaments?" you ask. Yes, the Mosaic economy, which set forth the truth by numerous symbols and ceremonies typifying Christ and his work, has changed. Christ came, thereby making the symbol and ceremony, the type itself, no longer necessary because the antitype and the reality itself had appeared. Moreover, the administration of the old covenant is not the current administration of the new, even while the content and substance of the spiritual blessings of both covenants remains progressively the same.

Conclusion

Our teaching and preaching will always remain stunted if we fail to see that God has a wholeness to his Word that embraces both testaments in one unified, single plan. The key that brings together both testaments arises naturally from the text itself, namely, the promise-plan of God.

Without a strong biblical theology component, such as the promise doctrine offers, the prospect of demonstrating great expositional preaching and teaching is very slim indeed. I recommend the appropriation and study of the diachronic scheme of the promise through the ages of biblical history as the best way to achieve such a biblical theology in preparation for doing expository preaching and teaching.[10]

3

The Task of Preaching and Teaching from the Old Testament Today

One of the oldest questions in the history of the church is this: What is the worth of the Old Testament to contemporary Christians? Is there any relevance, useful teaching, or continuity between the two testaments? Or is Christianity weighted down with its association with the Old Testament? Would the church be better off if it disregarded the Old Testament?

When one evaluates how much time is spent in some seminaries mastering what takes up over three-fourths of the whole Bible, that alone is enough to reconsider whether it is all that useful. Add to this the time spent in mastering the Hebrew language in other seminaries, and the conclusion seems self-evident.

But "the Old Testament problem . . . is not just one of many. It is the master problem of theology," warned Emil G. Kraeling.[1] Kraeling went on to observe that the commanding importance of the Old Testament runs through history like a scarlet thread. The reason is this: if one makes a mistake as it relates to the Old Testament, then it tends to trickle down into New Testament studies, theology, ethics, and practical Christian living. One needs only to be reminded of the second-century heretic Marcion to evaluate the full impact of the claim that making a wrong move with regard to the Old Testament affects everything else. His conclusions about the Old Testament had an impact on what he was able to extract from his expurgated New Testament and, consequently, a profound impact on his theology.

Where, then, shall we find any practical usefulness for the Old Testament? To be sure, the apostle Paul instructed young Timothy that the Old Testament was profitable and useful in 2 Timothy 3:16–17. But how is that to be taught, appreciated, and preached in today's world?

There are at least four main areas where the value of the Old Testament comes through quite clearly and where it is desperately needed in our day. The four areas are: doctrine, ethics, practical living, and preaching. Without the input of the Old Testament in each of these four areas, the church will find itself bankrupt in the twenty-first century.

There are a number of doctrines that come to their fullest expression in the Old Testament text. Some of the ones that come to mind are the doctrines of creation (Gen. 1–2), the fall (Gen. 3), the law of God (Exod. 20; Deut. 5), the incomparable greatness of God (Isa. 40), the nature of the substitutionary atonement of Christ (Isa. 52:13–53:12), the new heavens and the new earth (Isa. 65–66), and the second coming of our Lord to the Mount of Olives (Zech. 14). The point is this: if we avoid the Old Testament and depend solely on the New Testament, we will be providing the seedbeds for tomorrow's heresies, or in the merciful providence of God, an opportunity for a parachurch ministry to recover what others have neglected or deliberately bypassed.

We need not say much about our failure to preach on the law of God as rightly understood in the Old Testament. However, if all the ethical teaching we need is in the New Testament, as some object, then what shall we say to our generation about marrying close relatives, bestiality, and many of the new ethical and moral questions being posed in our day? The New Testament doesn't treat many of these subjects, for that testament presumes that we have read and heeded the older testament.

Closely aligned with this topic is the need for consistent practical living of the Christian life. Few sections of the Bible are so down-to-earth as the wisdom books. The worldwide demand for seminars on the family, on marriage, and on managing our finances proves that this may well be one of the most neglected areas in our preaching mission. And that is probably tied directly to our failure to preach as often as we should from the Old Testament. Where could one find a better theology of culture, leisure, and the management of material goods than in the book of Ecclesiastes? It teaches that all of life and its possessions—food, drink, paychecks, knowledge, and even spouses—are gifts from the hand of God.

But another unmet pressure point in today's world is the need for the strong prophetic announcement of the Word of God in our midst from the Old Testament. Modernity has reduced the clear exposition of the Word of God in all of its power to little more than topical essays on safe topics that do not tend to offend anyone. It is for this reason that I turn to this issue of preaching from the Old Testament.

Reasons Why the Church Should Hear the Old Testament

Let it be affirmed right away that the central theme of both the Old and New Testaments is Christ.[2] Did not our Lord rebuke the two disciples on the road to Emmaus on that first Easter Sunday afternoon for their failure to understand that he was the one to whom all the Law, Prophets, and Writings pointed (Luke 24:25–27)? Indeed, while the prophets were ignorant of the time and the circumstances surrounding the coming of the Messiah (1 Pet. 1:10–12), they were clear about five things: (1) they were writing about the Messiah; (2) they knew Messiah would suffer; (3) they knew Messiah would also be glorified and that he would triumph; (4) they knew the suffering would precede the glory; and (5) they knew that they were speaking not only to their own generation but to all of us who would come later, such as those in the church in Peter's day. Therefore, the prophets' bewilderment about their lack of knowledge as to the precise date of the appearing of Messiah should not be taken as proof that the prophets spoke "better than they knew," or that they often spoke in ignorance of what they wrote.

There are more reasons why the church should listen to the Old Testament. One could cite its sheer size, for some 77 percent of the Bible is found in the first thirty-nine books of the canon. Moreover, the content of the Old Testament is not basically one of law, as so many incorrectly think. Rather, it too is focused on the good news, the gospel, of our Lord Jesus Christ. This claim can be sustained by turning to Romans 1:1–2. In that text Paul argued that he had been "set apart for the gospel of God—the gospel [God] promised beforehand through his prophets in the Holy Scriptures." The "Holy Scripture" in Paul's day was none other than the Old Testament. And in that Old Testament the gospel was set forth long before Paul ever began to announce it!

The same argument is set forth in Hebrews 3:17–4:2. There the writer tells how the generation that perished in the wilderness did not enter into the Promised Land of Canaan because of their unbelief. That is why all of us should also be careful lest that same promise left to us of entering into God's place of rest should likewise be wasted. When the gospel is preached to us, just as the gospel was preached to those who died in the wilderness, we are in the same danger if we too do not believe that gospel. What is clear is that the same gospel preached in Moses' day is now being preached in our day!

One last reason must be listed here. Notice how many times the pronoun is changed from the third person, "he," "she," or "they," to "us," "we," or "our" when a citation is reiterated later in the Old Testament or in the New Testament. For example, God talked to Jacob in Genesis sometime around 1800 B.C. This same text is later used by the prophet Hosea in 700 B.C. He cited many of the same episodes and words from 1800 B.C. for that eighth century B.C. audience. In fact, the prophet Hosea argued that "[God] found [Jacob] at Bethel and there he talked with *us*" (Hosea 12:4, based on the Hebrew text; emphasis added). So God still was talking to later generations from the Genesis text written some 1,100 years earlier!

This same phenomenon occurs a dozen or more times in the New Testament. For example, Hebrews 6:18 argues that God affirmed his promise to Abraham by two unchangeable things: his word in Genesis 12 and his oath in Genesis 22. But he did this not only to give a strong assurance to Abraham but also to encourage us who live in New Testament times, "*we* who have fled to take hold of the hope offered to *us*" (emphasis added).

Therefore, that Old Testament text is addressed to us as much as it was addressed to Israel.

Reasons Why the Church Lost the Old Testament in Its Preaching

Few things will discourage the proper use of something more than abuse. That is what happened early in the history of the church. The attacks on the Old Testament by the heretic Marcion turned many away from the Old Testament. Prior to that Philo had begun a program of allegorical interpretation, just as some of the classical interpreters had done in order to retain the respectability of the gods and goddesses of the Greek and Roman religions by treating their religious texts of the Olympian pantheon allegorically. It was thought that everything on earth formed an analogy to something similar in heaven. Therefore, some scholars and pastors ceased trying to explain the difficult moral, ethical, and doctrinal issues raised by the Old Testament. These issues were quickly bypassed and exchanged for what were assumed to be their heavenly and spiritual counterparts. No one, however, was able to give divine authority for this doctrine of analogy or theory of correspondences that was said to exist between the earthly copy and the heavenly prototype.

Another practice in medieval and early reformation times was to assume that many, if not most, things in the Old Testament were types of something else in the New Testament. Now there are real types in the Bible, but all true biblical types have clear divine designations shown in the same contexts with the alleged type from the Old Testament. Consequently, a person, an institution, an act, or an event that can claim by divine designation in the Old Testament that it is a partial picture of a greater reality to come can be recognized by all true interpreters as a type. But the problem arises when everything in detail, such as all that is in the tabernacle, is made a type of something else. Surely, as one of my professors wisely remarked one day in class, some of the ropes and pegs in the tabernacle were meant to hold it up and to help it stand up erect! The problem with typology is that many take it far beyond what we have biblical authorization to do. Of course, there are more types in the Bible than what the New Testament claims to be types, but that is a long way from making most things in the Old Testament a type, especially by reading the Old Testament through the lens of the New Testament.

In a later move to demonstrate how the Old Testament can be made useful for contemporary believers, the Enlightenment declared that a biblical text was more important for *how* it was composed than for *what* it said. Supernatural words and events were also denied as a new rationalism took over where faith had once reigned. Moreover, the Word was atomized, fragmented, and generally lost for the preaching ministry of the church.

More recently the effects of postmodernity have been seen in systems of "reader response" hermeneutics. The meaning of a text has now shifted for many from the assertions of the human authors of Scripture, who stood in the council of God and received this revelation, to the meanings that the readers wish to attach to that text. This is little more than a modern form of eisegesis, "reading into" the text what the reader wishes to see there. This makes the Bible into a waxen nose that can be pushed in whichever direction one wishes it to go. It makes a mockery out of divine authority!

None of these systems helped us understand the Old Testament but were responsible for fostering a decline and loss of the message from the older testament in our churches and theological academies.

Reasons Why the Old Testament Helps One's Preaching

If we are to have a balanced and full ministry, we must preach the whole counsel of God (Acts 20:27) to the whole person. Neglect of any area of Scripture will provide the fertile soil for either heresy to grow in the church or, in the merciful providence of God, for a parachurch ministry to reclaim what has been neglected or deliberately set aside by the preaching ministry of the church.

Our teaching and preaching of the Old Testament must be balanced in its use of genre, encompassing all types of literature and emphases found in the Old Testament. Therefore it must include praise, but also lament; it must treat prose passages, but also poetic passages. As there are didactic texts, there are just as surely narratives. Sound, balanced teaching and preaching must include legal, proverbial, historical, eschatological, doctrinal, ethical, prophetic, wisdom, and apocalyptic texts from the older testament.

It can be said with confidence that without clear teaching from the Old Testament, the church and modern thought suffer. So many modern issues, such as the sanctity of truth, marriage, property, the heart and its motives, find their best undergirding and direction from the teaching of the Old Testament.

How Do We Preach from the Old Testament?

One of the greatest problems in teaching students and pastors how to use the Old Testament for contemporary preaching is learning how to cross the wide gulf that exists from the pre-Christian text to the twenty-first-century preaching situation. All too frequently the pastor is left to make this journey alone. Fortunately, more and more helps have been made available to pastors and teachers in recent times. I would like to briefly point to some of these as I conclude this introductory chapter.

A list of some of these resources in English may begin to establish the point that some help is beginning to appear.

For preaching Old Testament narrative:

Kaiser, Walter C., Jr. "Narrative," in *Cracking Old Testament Codes: A Guide to Interpreting the Literary Genres of the Old Testament*, ed. D. Brent Sandy and Ronald L. Giese Jr. (Nashville: Broadman and Holman, 1995), 69–88.

Matthews, Kenneth A. "Preaching Historical Narrative," in *Reclaiming the Prophetic Mantle: Preaching the Old Testament Faithfully*, ed. George L. Klein (Nashville: Broadman and Holman, 1992), 19–50.

Pratt, Richard L., Jr. *He Gave Us Stories: The Bible Student's Guide to Interpreting Old Testament Narrative* (Brentwood, Tenn.: Wolgemuth and Hyatt, 1990). A 500-page introduction for evangelicals.

For preaching Old Testament wisdom:

Garrett, Duane A. "Preaching Wisdom," in *Reclaiming the Prophetic Mantle*, 107–26.
McKenzie, Alyce M. *Preaching Proverbs: Wisdom for the Pulpit* (Louisville: Westminster/John Knox, 1996).

For preaching from the Old Testament Prophets:

Kaiser, Walter C., Jr. *Malachi: God's Unchanging Love* (Grand Rapids: Baker, 1984).
Kent, Dan G. "Preaching the Prophets," in *Reclaiming the Prophetic Mantle*, 93–105.
Smith, Gary V. *The Prophets as Preachers: An Introduction to the Hebrew Prophets* (Nashville: Broadman and Holman, 1994).
Ward, James, and Christine Ward. *Preaching from the Prophets* (Nashville: Abingdon, 1995).

For preaching from Old Testament Law:

Averbeck, Richard E. "Law," in *Cracking Old Testament Codes*, 113–38.
Bergen, Robert D. "Preaching Old Testament Law," in *Reclaiming the Prophetic Mantle*, 51–69.

For preaching from Old Testament apocalyptic:

Hanson, Paul D. *Old Testament Apocalyptic: Interpreting Biblical Texts* (Nashville: Abingdon, 1987).
Hewitt, C. M. Kempton. "Guidelines to the Interpretation of Daniel and Revelation," in *A Guide to Biblical Prophecy*,

ed. Carl E. Armerding and Ward W. Gasque (Peabody, Mass.: Hendrickson, 1989), 101–16.

Morris, Leon. *Apocalyptic* (Grand Rapids: Eerdmans, 1972).

Sandy, D. Brent, and Martin G. Abegg Jr. "Apocalyptic," in *Cracking Old Testament Codes*, 177–96.

There are more literary types, but this is enough of a sample to show that some progress has been made in helping the church get at the contemporary relevance of each of these literary genres of the Old Testament.

Conclusion

What hope is there that the Old Testament will be restored to its rightful place in the preaching mission of the church? There is great hope as a whole new series of helps are now being made available and as the seminary begins to assume its rightful share of the burden for helping the church find out how it can best succeed in this task.

Much of my efforts have gone into producing commentary that attempts to move beyond merely *what* the text said. Instead, I have tried to show *how* that same Old Testament text has contemporary application in the twenty-first century. Especially to be noted are my works on Psalms 120–34,[3] Micah to Malachi,[4] Lamentations,[5] Exodus,[6] and Leviticus.[7] But the task is far from finished. Together we must bend all our efforts to hear God's word from heaven out of the Old Testament as it speaks into our own day.

4

The Art and Science
of Expository Preaching

The cure for many of the ills afflicting the church and the seminaries of the day is to be found in the faithful exposition of the Word of God. Faithfulness in this area is the primary prerequisite for alleviating the deepest concerns currently held by the church and society.

Expository Preaching as the Solution

Many Bible teachers and preachers claim that what they do when they preach or teach can be called expository preaching/teaching. But this is not always the case. Expository teaching and preaching involves more than using a biblical passage as a springboard or point of reference in what otherwise could best be called a topical message. In fact, our teaching and preaching is so desperately weak at the present moment in the household of faith because of a scarcity of true biblical exposition.

So what is an expository sermon? An expository sermon or lesson is one that takes a minimum of a full paragraph (a scene in a narrative or a strophe in poetry) and allows the biblical text to supply both the shape and the content of the message or lesson from that text itself.[1]

The reason for this limitation is important. It is all too easy to fall into the trap of pouring what we already know of the grace of God into the different containers made up of different verses of Scripture without seriously giving each text an opportunity to first teach us what it wants to say. Not only does such preaching become repetitive, but it severely handicaps the preacher's opportunity to grow and stretch into new areas. And such stretching is all the more important when it comes to venturing into a new book of the Bible, especially when going into the Old Testament for a sermon or lesson.

A good case can be made for the fact that expository preaching is one of our oldest styles of preaching. Whether we are observing the Dead Sea community of Qumran, the rabbis in the early Christian era, or a more contemporary Donald Grey Barnhouse or John Stott, the common thread is exposition of the Scriptures. What separates topical preaching from expositional preaching, observed Ronald Allen, is that expository preaching and teaching unwaveringly begins and remains with the biblical text throughout the whole sermon.[2] Rather than beginning with a human need or concern as the impetus for the sermon, the expository sermon deliberately reverses the action and has the sermon originate in the exposition of the Biblical text itself. Exposition starts with the Biblical text and holds fast to that text throughout the sermon or lesson.

But how effective is such a strategy when it comes to announcing and expositing the Old Testament? Does it not raise special problems that are almost insurmountable for the contemporary speaker and audience? This is a large part of the reason why fewer teachers and pastors are using exposition as their preferred style, especially when they venture into the Old Testament.

Which Lens Shall We Use to Read the Old Testament?

Sidney Greidanus, in his very stimulating book *Preaching Christ from the Old Testament*, points to seven ways we can read and preach Christ from the Old Testament. They are the redemptive-historical progression, the promise-fulfillment method, the typological way, the analogical way, the longitudinal theme method, the contrast method, and the New Testament reference way.[3]

But Greidanus is absolutely clear that our purpose in preaching from the Old Testament is not to preach Christ to the exclusion of the "whole counsel of God." Instead, he insists, the preacher's task is "to view the whole counsel of God, with all its teachings, laws, prophecies, and visions, in the light of Jesus Christ."[4] He goes on to add an important qualifier:

> At the same time, it should be evident that we must not read the incarnate Christ *back* into the Old Testament text, which would be *eisegesis,* but we should look for legitimate ways of preaching Christ from the Old Testament in the *context of the New.*[5]

Therein he has stated the problem most precisely. The Bible was meant to be read forward, not backward. To read it backward is to end up with a flat Bible, one in which any mention of a topic calls for the total teaching in all Scripture to be used to interpret any one of the contributions made to that topic along the way. We will say more on this later in the chapter. But let us stay with the first question for now.

So what lens do we use to teach the whole counsel of God from the Old Testament? Will one of the seven methods (or each of the seven) discussed by Greidanus provide the proper insight into the Old Testament?

The place we must begin is with the plain, natural, original, historical meaning of the passage. If we ever abandon that as our starting point, we will have forfeited all hope for arriving at any agreed sense of meaning of a text.

Where Will I Find the Plain Sense of a Passage?

The only proper place to begin, then, is with the human author who claimed to obtain his meaning from being in the heavenly council of God. We do not attempt, however, to get at the author's psychological state of mind or anything of that sort. Rather, what we attempt to do is to understand the human author's use of words in the context of his life and times, literary genres, and theological givens.

Gordon Fee and Douglas Stuart stated it best when they said:

> The only proper control for hermeneutics is to be found in the original intent of the biblical text. . . . In contrast to . . . [pure] subjectivity, we insist that the original meaning of the text—as much as it is in our power to discern it—is the objective point of control.[6]

As for a text's historical background, we must first ask *what* did the author mean? What, in terms of his original usage of words, was the listeners' understanding of the words used when he spoke or wrote? What does an understanding of the history, the social and geographical settings, and the purpose of his writings contribute to our understanding of his message?

In the past, this approach has been known as the grammatical-historical interpretation of the text. The term "grammatical-historical interpretation" was used originally by Karl A. G. Keil.[7] The term "grammatical," however, is somewhat misleading in our ears today, for normally we mean the arrangement of words and the construction of sentences. But Keil did not have this meaning in mind when he used the term. Instead, he had in mind the Greek word *gramma*, which approximates what we would mean by the term "literal" (to use a synonym derived from Latin). Keil's grammatical sense was what we would call the simple, direct, plain, ordinary, natural, or literal sense of the phrases, clauses, and sentences.

Keil's use of "historical" meant that the interpreter had to consider these words in relation to the time, circumstances, events, and persons in that historical period in which the author wrote. Thus, the grand object for Keil, as it is for us, was to ascertain the *usus loquendi*, that is, the specific use of the words as they were employed by the writer under consideration and/or as prevalent in the day and age in which he wrote.[8]

Does the Literary Form of a Passage Affect Its Meaning?

To further narrow the scope of the author's possible meanings, we must ask, *How* does this text take on its meaning? In other words, what genre or literary format did the author use? Did the writer use an expositional prose, a narrative, a praise form, a lament, or a prophetic or proverbial form to encapsulate his ideas? Each of these formats will entail a different interpretive strategy. Each of these strategies will be discussed in the chapters that follow.

Ronald Allen's essay in Wardlow's 1983 book titled *Preaching Biblically*[9] may have been one of the first books to call our attention to how the shape or literary genre of a biblical passage needs to be reflected in the sermon. It suddenly became clear that most of us automatically change our rules of interpretation when we read a newspaper and move from the editorial page, to advertisements, to comic strips, and to letters to the editor. Each genre in the newspaper has its own special set of guidelines that demands adjustments in our way of handling the text. The Bible likewise must be read with a sensitivity to such changes in the literary genres.

Each genre embodies characteristic literary patterns that are unique to that particular form. Literary forms carry with them special effects for the reader or listener that signal a particular set of conditions for interpreting that form. Parables are not to be read as laments or psalms of praise. Neither is an apocalyptic genre to be read as a narrative or miracle genre. The fine-tuning of these distinctions is what we purpose to do in the chapters that follow.

What Gives Unity to an Expository Sermon?

An expository sermon cannot be defined as such merely by the fact that Hebrew, Greek, or Aramaic words are parsed, phrases are examined, and various geographical, historical, or archaeological features in the biblical text are brought out in our public explanations. Unfortunately, students too often recall what was done in some of their seminary exegesis classes and confuse this with biblical exposition. Such a method usually lacks a concept of unity and an integrating theme that has been found in the passage itself.

So, even after we have determined *what* a passage meant and *how* that meaning was conveyed in its day as well as in ours, the question still remains: Are there other lenses we must use to further sharpen our focus?

Yes, there are other lenses from which we can view this text. First of all, words or sentences cannot be unpacked as if they were isolated packages with meanings in and of themselves. Just because these words represent the truth of God, we cannot treat them in a fractured, isolated, or mysterious way that confers deep theological meanings that we import from other parts of the Scriptures. Therefore, I will suggest some ordinary steps that will help guide our movement from understanding what a text meant all the way up to applying what it means today.

Find the Extent of the Pericope

Words belong to sentences, and sentences usually belong to paragraphs, scenes, strophes, or larger units within the grammar of a genre. This is why I urge that a good expositional sermon never take *less* than a full paragraph, or its literary equivalent (e.g., a scene, a strophe, or the like), as a basis. The reason is clear: Only the full paragraph, or its equivalent, contains one full idea or concept of that text. To split off some of its parts is to play with the text as if it could be bent in any fashion in order to accomplish what we think is best.

Therefore, we must find the extent of the whole pericope. The pericope is the full story in each episode in the narrative, or the whole poem, to which each of the paragraphs, scenes, or strophes contributes. Again, our desire is to achieve wholeness, completeness, and the end to which each paragraph, scene, or strophe contributes to the whole or unified idea of each teaching block of text (pericope). Often this wholeness may encompass a full chapter in the Bible. At other times the pericope will extend only for a full paragraph or just part of a chapter of the Bible.[10]

The sermon, then, is anchored in the meaning first given to the text by the author. This meaning is further signaled by the literary genre that encapsulates the original message of the text. It is further limited by the extent of the teaching block or pericope that goes to make up the sections of the book.

Find the Focal Point of the Passage

Now we must find the "focal point" of that pericope, or the pivotal point in the passage. This pivotal point is where the passage's theme or point of view comes out in its fullest expression. This may be a single statement, a single verse, or sometimes a full clause somewhere within the pericope under study.

This focal point supplies one of the key components of expository preaching: the "unifying theme or topic" that the sermon and the text share. Here is where the whole point, or what Haddon Robinson calls the "Big Idea," of the biblical text and the sermon can be reduced to a single statement or announcement of a theme. This is what makes the message cohere and prevents a random walking about in the biblical passage that trails off into unrelated themes and ideas. In short, the title or topic for our message is found in this focal point that now serves as the unifying factor in the sermon. It must simultaneously be present in the biblical text being studied and be the dominant theme or subject of the message.

The reason for this limitation is important. It is all too easy to fall into the trap of imposing upon the different verses of Scripture what we already know of the grace of God without giving each text an opportunity to first teach us what it wants to say.

What separates topical preaching from expositional preaching, as we have already observed from Ronald Allen,[11] is that it unwaveringly begins and remains with the biblical text. The identification of the focal point of the passage will keep the sermon and the preacher focused on the real topic being presented in the Word of God. We now have a title or a subject for our exposition and sermon.

Find the Homiletical Key Word

By carefully observing all the connecting or transitional words (conjunctions, prepositions, and even adverbs) that appear with some frequency in the pericope, one can determine the homiletical key word for this entire passage. But how does one go about doing this?

First of all, this homiletical key word must name something that is found in each of the paragraphs or their literary equivalents. That is, we must use a noun to express the connections that we observe in this entire passage. But it must not be just any noun; it must be an abstract noun, for we wish to state what is in this passage in the form of a principle so that it can apply to all times and all places. And since we are usually going to have more than one principle, it is best that we use a plural abstract noun that will be able to align all the major points of the sermon in a clear explication of the title or subject we have discovered as the focal point of the Scripture text.

First, see if the passage under examination exhibits a series of transitional or connective words, such as a series of "ifs," yielding a homiletical key word of "conditions," or a series of "sinces," yielding a homiletical key word of "concessions," or "becauses" yielding a homiletical key word of "reasons."

Another approach is to repeat the title or subject of the passage and then ask: What is being said about this subject in this text? Take each paragraph (scene or strophe) and arrange the topic sentence of each one so that you can see the development or connection as you progress through the pericope. After you have written out the theme or topic sentence of each paragraph (scene or strophe), then ask what type of action they share. Are all of the paragraphs giving us ways to accomplish what was in the subject? Or are these paragraphs setting forth truths or principles for our edification? If you still are stuck, then proceed to the next step.

Find the Interrogative

There are six interrogatives that frequently will help us to discover how the paragraphs within the pericope are related. Five begin with a *w:* Who? What? Why? Where? and When? The sixth one is How? Thus, I can repeat the subject or title of my message that I derived from the focal point and then ask which of these interrogatives shows what unifies all the points around the central affirmation made in the focal point.

"Who" points to persons, "what" points to truths and the like, "why" to reasons, "where" to places, "when" to times or situations, and "how" often leads to ways.

The point is that these six interrogatives can assist the preacher in determining the organizing center for the passage. No doubt, there are other types of questions one could ask about what unifies the text. But the easiest and simplest way to begin is to use one of these six interrogatives. Is it a who, a what, a where, a when, a why, or a how that is being talked about in this text?

Make the Main Points Relevant and Contemporary

Now that the title or subject for the message is fixed and the whole passage is related to a plural abstract noun that feeds off an interrogative, it is time to organize the outline for your message. The temptation now will be to leave the text in its pre-Christian or first-century clothing. But that is exactly what has given expository preaching its bad reputation of being as dry as a dreary history lesson or as boring as a story about someone else's relatives!

There are a few hints that, if followed to the letter, can assist the preacher or teacher in this situation. First, avoid all use of proper names in the outline except for any of God's names. This means that there must be no references to any of the heroes of the Bible and no references to the cities, nations, territories, or the like in the outline of the sermon. All of that immediately dates the outline and pulls it away from being a contemporary word to people of today.

Second, never use the past tense of any verb in your sermon outline. This is another dead giveaway that we are thinking more about "back then" than we are about people now.

Third, we must not use third-person pronouns (*they, them, it, she, he,* or even *that* and *those*), for each third-person pronoun places the listener in the position of being outside the action and merely listening in on it.

On the positive side, we should use God's name in the sermon outline. In fact, whenever we are at a loss as to what we should preach on a passage, we will never go wrong if we focus on God, his actions and his requirements. But when the names of Israel, Moses, Isaiah, or David are found in a sermon outline, they reveal that we are preaching a B.C. sermon and not a twenty-first-century message.

Rather than using past tenses of the verbs in our outlines, we should use imperatives or present tense verbs. In fact, we may use almost any other verb form except the past tense if we still wish to communicate to a contemporary audience.

Finally, whereas I have seriously warned about the use of third-person pronouns, I would recommend that we use first-person plural pronouns (*us, we, our*) in the main points of our sermon. Of course, one could use second-person pronouns as well, but I have found that it is more humble and befitting our high office if we identify with the people to whom we preach, rather than piling on them injunctions as if we and God were on high now demanding that they, in contradistinction to God and us, should change in light of what is being said. So use the first-person plural pronouns—"Let *us*, brethren," "it is *our* job, brethren," and so on.

Conclude the Sermon by Making a Final Appeal

Frequently we are too rushed at the end of the exposition to do more than hastily wrap up our points. Worse still is the practice of offering a prayer at the end of our preaching that reviews the points one by one, apparently to give the Lord time to go over our points as a review, for he is the one to whom we are now offering the prayer!

Far better is the practice of working hard to ascertain where it is that the Holy Spirit would have us call for decisive action based upon the truth of what we have just preached. This does not come easily for most of us. It may take anywhere from forty-five minutes to an hour and a half of earnest preparation to conclude how we should issue the summons to the congregation to change their ways and deeds and to respond to what this particular Scripture wants us to do and be. Often, I have to pray through this aspect of the preparation or have my heart and soul stirred by listening to Handel's *Messiah* in order for me to take the principles I had announced in my main points and set them as challenges for action—things I had to *do* if I was to be faithful in my response to the text.

Therefore, the conclusion is one of the most critical parts of a message. I must issue a royal (i.e., a divine) summons to specific suggestions for immediate action. There must be a call for God to change us in light of the purity of his Word. But there must also be a caution here: I must call for specific actions that are based uniquely on what is precisely taught in this passage. All too frequently we call for generically true actions that could have been found in a hundred other passages—but, unfortunately, not in the one being preached at this time. So be careful that the challenge is found in this text.

One other caution. Evangelicals in particular are known for leaving messages at the cognitive level. We often think we have done our job when we have asked God's people to "think about this," or "believe this," or "remember this." But it suddenly struck me one day that Beelzebub could respond just as well to my sermons if that was all I was asking people to do. The devil believes all of these things and more. He knows they are true; he just doesn't *act* on any of these claims. Thus, we must call for action. Perhaps this is why up to 30 percent of Americans will say they have had a born-again experience with God or at least some kind of personal experience with God, but we see so little Christian impact on the culture. It may be that their "faith" is all too cerebral and is not put into action and reflected in a change of living or acting.

Conclusion

Expository preaching is not one of the optional luxuries of the pulpit. In fact, it remains one of the most earnestly desired skills among pastors according to recent polls. The seriousness of the times and the authority of the Word of God demand that we strive with all the fervor of our beings to see this skill developed in our ministries if we are to sense once again what God meant for the church to be and experience.

Part 2

How to Preach and Teach from the Old Testament

5

Preaching and Teaching Narrative Texts of the Old Testament

One of the first books to call our attention to the importance of the form of the text of Scripture was a book published in 1983 titled *Preaching Biblically*.[1] This book noted how the form of the sermon might be affected and actually helped by beginning with the *form* of the biblical text. That same spirit motivates the work we now take up in this and the succeeding chapters.

Narrative is the preferred genre of the biblical text. According to one way of counting, narrative could make up half of the corpus of both testaments. This is because the heart of the message of the Scriptures is itself the story of the redemptive plan of God.

But there is more to this preference for narrative than immediately meets the eye. Note how many people in the pews on Sunday morning seem to have their interests revived when an anecdote or story is interjected into the message. Heads that had been bent over suddenly pop up, and a sea of faces once again greets the preacher as the story is unfolded. Ever since we were children, almost all of us have loved to hear or tell a story. It should come as no surprise, therefore, when the most important disclosure ever to be made to mortals should also employ this same strategy for some of the very same reasons.

In order to properly prepare for teaching or preaching on narratives, it is necessary to understand how narratives are put together and how they work. Such an investigation of narrative technique will help us to slow down in our examination of the text and in our desire to get to the end or the point of the story. In this way we will be more observant of the smaller, but important, details of the narrative. It will likewise protect us from over-interpreting the text by filling in the narrative gaps with our own imagination and treating that filler as if it were the same as the text of Scripture.

The Elements in Narrative Texts

A narrative, by its very nature, "requires a story and a storyteller."[2] The narrator may tell the story in either a first-person or third-person style. When the first person is used, the "I" of the story can relate what happened from the standpoint of what the narrator experienced or observed. But when the third person, "he," "she," or "they," is used, the story can take a number of different perspectives, and as a result the story may more easily jump from place to place or from one time to another. The biblical narrators tend to prefer third-person narration, which provides them greater freedom in giving the wider picture of what is going on in the story.

The central elements in the total package of literary devices used in narrative include: (1) scene, (2) plot, (3) point of view, (4) characterization, (5) setting, (6) dialogue, (7) *leitwort*, or keywording, (8) structure, and (9) stylistic and rhetorical literary devices employed. It is from this wide repertoire that the storyteller draws as the narrative is committed to writing.

Scene

"In the Old Testament prose," declared J. P. Fokkelmann, "the scene is about the most important unit in the architecture of the narrative."[3] Each scene represents something that took place at some particular time or place. In this regard, then, the scene acts much as the paragraph does in regular prose writing, usually supplying one main idea for each scene. That will be a great help to the teacher or homiletician who is struggling to show how the narrative goes together in its own inner logic and how legitimate principles may be derived from that text.

Therefore, whenever a narrative indicates a change in time or place, it is at that point one may mark off a new scene and therefore what is equivalent to a new paragraph and a new thought that is being built within the logic and structure of the story. Several Bible versions will indicate more breaks in the text, for their rule is to indent and begin a new paragraph every time the speaker changes. But this rule usually is not useful for scene analysis and for preaching. Instead, we should stick with the general rule that scenes change only when the time or place changes.

Each scene is usually made up of two or more characters. In those cases where a group appears in a scene, it functions as one of the characters. However, for biblical narrative, one of the most distinguishing features is what Sidney Greidanus calls "the pervasive presence of God" in these scenes.[4] Greidanus goes on to note that more often than not, God is one of the two characters in these scenes. However, even when God is not mentioned directly, his presence is often implied by the very point of view taken by the narrator.

The task of the interpreter, teacher, or preacher, then, is to begin the study of each narrative by marking off the scenes in each story. This process is similar to the way one would break up a prose passage by marking off the individual paragraphs. Once these divisions are made, it is helpful to compose in one's own words a brief synopsis of what is being said or happening in each scene, for this will function much like the topic or theme sentence functions in prose paragraphs. In this way, the interpreter will focus on the narrative itself, allowing the form of the story as it now appears in the text to set the agenda of ideas to be attached to it. Such a constructive reading of the text avoids the inconsistencies of a deconstructive or imposed ideological overlay on the text.

A good illustration of the use of scenes can be found in stories as diverse as the call of Samuel in 1 Samuel 3 or the beginning of the ministry of Elijah in 1 Kings 17. In the case of the story about Samuel, the text exhibits a change in scene by the shift in time, which may be analyzed as follows:

I. Previous Days—1 Samuel 3:1 ("In those days the word of the LORD was rare")

II. One Night—1 Samuel 3:2–14
III. Next Morning—1 Samuel 3:15–18
IV. Subsequent Days—1 Samuel 3:19–4:1a

Each of these scenes will become the basis for a major point, or Roman numeral, in the message that is developed from these four scenes. It will be necessary to limit each scene to one major idea that develops the central idea of the passage in successive thoughts in the progress of the whole story.

A similar illustration of the change in scenes can be shown in the shift in place seen in 1 Kings 17:

I. The Palace—1 Kings 17:1
II. The Brook and Revine Kerith—1 Kings 17:2–7
III. The City Gate of Zarephath—1 Kings 17:8–16
IV. In the House of the Zarephath Widow—1 Kings 17:17–24

A change in the time and place determines where to make the breaks in a narrative text for the preparation of the text for proclamation. It is that simple and that definite. These scenes will function now for the sermon much in the same way that paragraphs function in a prose passage of the Bible.

Plot

The plot is what gives movement to the story, for each narrative must have a beginning, a middle or midpoint, and an end. This sequencing we call the plot. It traces the movement of the events and episodes as they emerge in the story. The plot must move toward a climax and some type of resolution. Involved in the concept of the plot is the relationship that exists between a sequence of events and the causes and consequences that are related to that sequence.

Some plots carry a complex format, but most biblical plots employ a single plot forming a "classical pyramid pattern."[5] From a peaceful initial situation, the action builds toward a climax until it drops off again to a tranquil situation. Bar-Efrat illustrated this pyramid pattern from Genesis 22, where the story begins with God's quiet request for Abraham to sacrifice Isaac.

The action crests with the near-sacrifice of Isaac and then settles back down as the boy and his father descend Mount Moriah.

A more complex illustration, from Bar-Efrat, is the story of Isaac's blessing of Jacob in Genesis 27. The action climaxes when Isaac almost discovers the ruse his son is pulling on him. The action subsides as Isaac blesses Jacob, who is pretending to be Esau. But another climax is immediately encountered when Esau enters and requests his father's blessing, which has just been given away. A new resting point in the action of the story is reached when Jacob leaves his home and some distance is put between the hostile brothers.

Point of View

Point of view refers to the perspective from which the story is told. Usually it is the prerogative of the narrator to express the stance or viewpoint from which the story is being told. Occasionally, the narrator yields that privileged position and allows one of the characters in the narrative to make the point that is desired in the story. For example, the writer of 1 Kings 17 allowed the final speech of the Zarephath widow to give the point of view of the four preceding scenes and thus the whole point of the story. She said, "Now I know that you are a man of God and that the word of the LORD from your mouth is the truth" (1 Kings 17:24).

The point of view gives coherence to the whole series of joined episodes or scenes. Once we have identified that verse or portion of a verse in the narrative that supplies the point of view for the entire group of scenes, we are able to declare what the subject of this passage is and the title we will be able to give to our message. In the case of the widow's statement, we can assert that this passage of 1 Kings 17 is about "Finding That the Word of the Lord Is Dependable and True."[6]

Thus the point of view supplies the lens through which the reader, interpreter, and expositor may relate to the acts or events of each scene. In this way the basis for preaching and teaching from a narrative passage begins to build before our eyes. Once we have set off the scenes, noted how the plot develops, and identified the point of view found within the passage, we are well on our way to using the expositional method of preaching from narratives.

It must be noted, however, that it is possible to misunderstand what is meant by point of view. After all, every person potentially can express a number of personal points of view, even on the same subject. But that cannot be done with integrity here while still claiming the authority of the text or the divine voice from heaven. One could speak of a psychological viewpoint, an ideological viewpoint, a temporal viewpoint, or even of the perspective from the various rhetorical devices used in a narrative. But none of these can compete with the viewpoint that the original writer, who stood in the council of God and received the original revelation, has expressed in the text of this passage. The text is no more divided against itself than is the divine mind that inspired the text in the first place. There may be a number of aspects that are of interest as supporting roles are identified in the point of view offered in the passage, but that is all they are—supporting or supplementing viewpoints that reinforce the dominant theme of the story. Only when the point of view is left unexpressed and is merely implied (as happens in a few cases) will the point of view be difficult to assert. In those cases we must depend on other elements in the narrative to help us reconstruct the author's point of view, and thus the subject or title of our message.

Characterization

Once an analysis of the way a narrative is structured has been secured, it is important to begin discovering what a narrative expresses. The substance of what a narrative portrays can be found especially clearly in its use of character.

The real movement of a narrative comes from the characters and their actions and speeches. Therefore, it is just as impossible to portray a character apart from the events as it is to depict the events as separate from the character.

Richard Bowman notes that character in the biblical narratives is set forth in four different ways:

1. through a character's own actions and his or her interactions with other characters,
2. through a character's own speeches,
3. through the speeches of other characters about a specific character, and
4. through the narrator's specific comments about a character.[7]

While the Old Testament rarely describes its characters, it prefers to give the briefest physical, gentilic, or professional designations. For instance, Saul is "a head taller than any of the others" (1 Sam. 9:2), while others may simply be an Amalekite, Amorite, Hittite, prophet, prostitute, or shepherd. Enough is given to locate them with reference to the point of the story but never enough detail to satisfy our curiosity. Seldom does the biblical text indulge in the psychology of the characters, but it may describe moral or intellectual traits. Thus Jacob is "the deceiver," while Nabal is "the fool." All of this stands in contrast to Homer's *Iliad* and *Odyssey*, where the heroes are given rather full descriptions.

How, then, are we to determine characterization in biblical narratives if it is used so sparingly? The answer is this: Characterization may be detected mainly through the actions and dialogues of the narrative's participants. One must be especially observant when considering dialogue in this regard. This is the chief way that narrative sets forth its character. Moreover, one will often encounter many aspects in one and the same character. Thus, we will see both the strengths and weaknesses of the patriarchs, the kings of Israel, and even the prophets and priests of Israel.

Characterizations may be either static or dynamic. When a biblical character does not change throughout the entire story, that character may be described as static. But when a character shows considerable change and development during the course of the story, that one may be labeled dynamic. The first judge in the Book of Judges is Othniel, who in the course of his judgeship goes to war with Aram and is successful. More than that we cannot say, so he must be regarded as a static character. On the other hand, Samson is a very complex and multifaceted character. Despite his prenatal appointment to be a Nazarite from birth and a deliverer of Israel, he wastes his youth in courting Philistine women, only to be betrayed by his paramours.

Often characters are played off against each other, thus giving us a better idea of both by way of contrasts. For example, Rahab stands over against Achan in the Book of Joshua, while Samuel is a strong contrast to the sons of Eli. Surely Saul is the reverse of David, and Ruth is the opposite of Orpah. In this way, some of these characters act as foils.

The central character of the Bible is God. This comes as no surprise, for in almost every narrative God is present explicitly or by implication. Therefore, the interpreter's and expositor's attention must be centered on God's role in the narrative. This reminds us that all efforts to concentrate on the human character in a story while failing to locate God's actions in the narrative are wrong. It leads to divorcing the character from God's larger redemptive plan, bypassing the point that the author was making. Accordingly, one of our key questions in determining the characterization of a narrative is: What is God doing in this scene? What is the writer of this Scripture trying to say in this narrative by his particular point of view as it fits in with his total purpose for writing? The expositor must not be distracted by temptations to be reductionistic or to develop one's own sets of moralisms, good as they may be or as frequently as they may be taught somewhere else in the Bible.

Setting

It is important to locate the plot and the characters in the space/time world they inhabit. It is no secret that biblical narrative is closely related to history, for that is one of its categories: historical narrative.

But setting has other functions as well. When the story of the sacrifice of Isaac is set on Mount Moriah in Genesis 22, this is not a throwaway detail that has no function or import to the story. On the contrary, this story, and this fact in particular, prepares us for the fact that on this same spot the temple mount will be built and future sacrifices will take place. This becomes clear through later revelation when 2 Chronicles 3:1, almost in a matter-of-fact way, announces, "Then Solomon began to build the temple of the LORD in Jerusalem on Mount Moriah." This point can be brought out as we summarize the teaching of this passage with the theology of the whole Bible. The fact that the Elijah narrative is set in the reign of King Ahab and Queen Jezebel is likewise important to understanding the background against which his protest against polytheism was aimed. Moreover, Jezebel's father was king of Sidon, a source of Canaanite influence against which the prophet raised his holy objections. Setting, then, can add a significant factor to the interpreter's understanding of a story.

Dialogue

If characterization is somewhat rare in the stories of the Old Testament, the exact opposite can be said of the use of dialogue in these narratives. As Robert Alter observed so well,

> Everything in the world of biblical narrative ultimately gravitates towards dialogue. Quantitatively, a remarkably large part of the narrative burden is carried by dialogue, the transactions between characters typically unfolding through words they exchange, with only the most minimal intervention of the narrator.[8]

Dialogue plays such a central part that one can often find in the speech of one of the leading persons in the narrative the point of view of the whole passage. For example, we have already seen how in 1 Kings 17:24 the writer avoids saying directly in his own words what he wishes to say. Instead, the writer resorts to having the widow conclude in her own words: "Now I know that you are a man of God and that the word of the LORD from your mouth is the truth." Therein lies the difference between expositional prose writing, which is *direct* in its assertions, and narrative telling, which by its very nature utilizes an *indirect* means of making its assertions. But one must not conclude that because the direct method of stating things is avoided the writer does not have just as clear and certain a point to make in the narrative.

Alter supplies two very helpful rules about the use of dialogue when interpreting narrative:

- Note the place where the dialogue is first introduced, for that often is the important moment in revealing the character of the speaker—perhaps even more important than in the substance of what is said!
- Note also where the narrator has chosen to introduce dialogue instead of narration. That rhythm of moving back and forth between narrative and dialogue is part of the effect that is being created. And in the sharp exchange between the characters, light will be shed on the relationship of the characters to God and to each other.[9]

It is especially important to pay attention to those times when one character repeats a part or the whole of what another has just said. Often in these repetitions, there is a small deviation, slight alteration, reversal of order, elaboration, deletion, or another difference. Such may tip off the interpreter to something that may be a key to disclosing the character or event being described.

Some examples of this variation in dialogue may help. The oldest example is the one where God's instructions to Adam concerning the trees of the garden (Gen. 2:15–17) are repeated with slight differences by the serpent and the woman, thereby giving their own twist to the commands of God (Gen. 3:1–2). Likewise, the commands of the three army captains of fifty men who were sent to Elijah the prophet show a development as the last two know that the previous platoon of fifty had been suddenly destroyed by a word from the mouth of the prophet (2 Kings 1:9–15). They move from "Man of God, the king says, 'Get down!'" (v. 9) to "Man of God, this is what the king says, 'Get down at once!'" (v. 11), with the final form being, "Man of God, please have respect for my life and the lives of these fifty men, your servants! Look, the fire has fallen from heaven [God] and consumed the first two captains and all their men. But now have respect for my life!" (vv. 13–14, my translation).

The rather remarkable thing about dialogue in the Bible is that it is always between two characters or groups, and rarely between three or more. But it is dialogue that adds color, vividness, and realism to biblical narrative, thus making the truth taught all the more memorable.

Leitwort, *or Key-wording*

Often the story will use the same word or a pattern of words related in sound or form at important points in the narrative. In this case, these words may be used to stress the thematic unity of the entire pericope or to set forth a motif in the story. Thus, prominence is given to a word or set of words because of its frequency of use or the way it is strategically employed. Kenneth Matthews shows how Genesis 22 has a threefold iteration of "your son, your only son" (Gen. 22:2, 12, 16) within this narrative.[10] This is another way of emphasizing that the boy is a most important aspect of this story. Another illustration is the frequent use of "house" (for "dynasty") in 2 Samuel 7, where God promises to build a dynasty out of David rather than have David build a house for him.

Robert Alter has revived an old example of a key word to explain how Genesis 37 is connected to Genesis 38, for on most accounts it would appear that the latter chapter is an interruption of the otherwise uniform narrative of Joseph.[11] However, when one considers the juxtaposition of the *Leitworten* "kid" or "young goat" and the verb "to recognize" in the two stories (37:31, 33; 38:17, 25–26), a most startling discovery can be made. Just as the kid was used by Joseph's brothers to deceive their father Jacob into believing Joseph had died, perhaps in an attack by a wild animal, so Judah (the one who suggested that the brothers sell Joseph to the Midianites) was himself deceived by his aggrieved daughter-in-law. He finally "recognized," in a most embarrassing moment, why the "kid" goat was never delivered to the woman he had accosted! This is but another form of repetition used in biblical narrative.

Structure

Hebrew narratives exhibit structures that are a "network of relations among the parts of an object or a unit."[12] Since every narrative has some type of deliberate arrangement of all its parts, it is important to examine how those parts fit together and interrelate. In this way not only will the unity of the story become apparent, but its themes, emphases, and plot also will be uncovered.

The most natural part of structure to observe is the climax to a story. This is its denouement or peak, which usually serves as the focus of the story as well. Accordingly, the Joseph story rises to its high point when Joseph reveals who he is to his brothers in Genesis 43–45.

In other narratives, such as the story of Job, the structure can be gained from recurring phrases. For example, Job 1:13–19 is punctuated with the recurring word from the four messengers who each came, "while [the other] was still speaking," and said, after relating their tragic news: "I am the only one who has escaped to tell you."

But there is also a larger structure that ties together a complex of narratives. Thus, we have the Abrahamic cycle (Gen. 11:27–25:11), the Joseph cycle (Gen. 37–50), the Samuel cycle (1 Sam. 1–16), and the Elijah and Elisha cycle (1 Kings 17–2 Kings 13). Here it is important to notice how each individual pericope within the larger structure contributes and expands the theme of the whole structure as well as the individual structure. In the case of the Elijah and Elisha cycle, it would appear that 2 Kings 2:14 is the denouement. With the translation of Elijah to heaven in a whirlwind, the question is asked rhetorically, "Where is the LORD God of Elijah?" (KJV). In this way the power of God can be viewed in each episode of these two prophets. First Kings 17 demonstrates the power of God's word. First Kings 18 shows the power of God in action as fire comes down from heaven. In the next episode, 1 Kings 19, God's power is seen in his ability to restore his servant from emotional and spiritual collapse. But it is all part of the power of God.

Stylistic and Rhetorical Devices in Narrative

In the words that each author chooses, there is evidence of the writer's own style. A few of the ways that style may be evidenced is by noting what is repeated and what is omitted, as well as the author's use of chiasm, irony, and similar figures of speech. Each of these rhetorical devices is worthy of brief discussion.

REPETITION

Already we have highlighted the use of a key word, or *leitwort.* Besides this form of repetition, one can also see what appear to Westerners as redundancies. However, it may well be that these repetitions supply the very genius of that story in making the emphasis that needs to be made.

In addition to providing the emphasis for the narrative, repetition may provide the beginning and ending of that pericope. This is what we call *inclusio,* a form of bracketing in which the start and finish of a block of material is indicated by the use of the same words or phrases. In this way, the appendix to the Book of Judges is marked off. It says, "In those days there was no king in Israel: every man did that which was right in his own eyes" (Judg. 17:6 and 21:25 KJV).

Surprisingly, this same formula appears in a modified form within the unit itself in Judges 18:1 and 19:1, thereby tying together the larger structure with the units within that macrostructure.[13] Another such instance is the structure supplied by the author of Genesis for his book: "This is the account [history, generations] of . . ." (Gen. 2:4; 5:1; 6:9; 10:1; 11:10, 27; 25:12, 19; 36:1, 9; 37:2), thereby providing eleven blocks of material.

Finally, repetition can point to aspects of a person's character. One need only note the slight variations in a divine command that is repeated to detect flaws in a person's character. In this way we are tipped off as to the character of the serpent and the woman when they repeat the prohibition of God about the trees in the Garden of Eden, but with their own twist (Gen. 2:15–17; 3:1–2). Such care in reading and interpreting the text often yields great insights into the character of those we are dealing with, even though the Hebrew text usually offers very little by way of characterization.

OMISSIONS

Just as important as the repetitions are the omissions of a text. Sometimes there are unstated pieces of information that are essential for getting at the meaning of a passage. These "gaps" or "systems of gaps," as Meir Sternberg labeled them,[14] play an important role in the narrative.

GUIDELINES FOR INTERPRETING NARRATIVE

1. First, identify each scene of the narrative. Every time there is a change in the time or place, there is a change in scene. These scenes will make up the main points in your message.
2. Analyze the plot of the passage. Watch the action move from the start to the climax and denouement and then back down to its conclusion. This should give you the beginning, middle, and end of the narrative.
3. Determine the point of view of the narrative. Where does the text come to a focal point so that the subject of the passage and the title of your message become clear?
4. Watch how the author uses his dialogue and special figures of speech to carry out the point of view expressed in each of the scenes.
5. Note how the scenes are related to each other through the point of view or subject of the entire narrative.
6. Note what stylistic devices are used in order to detect the proper emphasis, characterization, and so on.

One must be careful at this point not to read into the narrative what may not have been intended. Many deconstructionists have exaggerated the role of omissions to introduce what is basically foreign to the story and its intentions. But there are natural questions that do arise that may reveal an unstated motive. For example, in the case of David's soldier, Uriah, why did he not go home to sleep with his wife when he was called back from the fighting lines? Was his concern with the provisions of holy war? Or did he suspect David and his wife Bathsheba already? These questions have no real answer, but the very fact that the text leaves a gap here makes us think all the more about the motives of Uriah.

Chiasm

Chiasm is a literary device named after the Greek letter *chi*, which looks and functions like our *x*. It involves the crossing or inverting of related elements in parallel constructions, whether words, clauses, parallel lines of poetry, or a whole narrative.[15] This figure of speech is closely related to key-wording, climax, denouement, and inclusion. In a set of chiastic lines, the first and last ideas parallel each other while the middle pair of ideas are also balanced and parallel to one another.

IRONY

Irony is a special form of speech in which the writer says the exact opposite of what he or she intends. Elijah masterfully used this type of talk when he made his suggestions to the Baal worshipers as to why Baal had not yet been able to make an appearance (1 Kings 18:27). Job, likewise, says ironically to his three so-called comforters, "Doubtless you are the people, and wisdom will die with you!" (Job 12:1).

Such words, which function much as hyperbole, tend to magnify an object beyond reality for the express purpose of showing how the true state of affairs is exactly the opposite.

An Illustration of Preaching a Narrative Text: 1 Samuel 3:1–4:1a

The text is 1 Samuel 3:1–4:1a. It is entitled, "The Power of the Word of God." This title comes from the focal point found in 1 Samuel 3:19—"[God] let none of his words fall to the ground." Our major points will follow the four scenes that were mentioned above: (1) The Previous Days, v. 1; (2) One Night, vv. 2–14; (3) Next Morning, vv. 15–18; and (4) Subsequent Days, vv. 19–4:1a. I believe that this text informs us as to *what* (the interrogative for our message) are the *characteristics* (our homiletical key word) that demonstrate the power of the Word of God to this very day.

Let us examine the exposition of this text as a typical Sunday audience would hear it.

The motto of Geneva, Switzerland in the early 1500s was "After darkness, light!" It was a bold affirmation of Calvin and his generation that "light" came to God's people through the preaching of God's Word. Therefore, in order for the darkness of that town to be dispelled, six sermons from the Bible were mandated for each citizen each week. One sermon was to come at dawn on Sunday and another at the usual hour of 9 A.M. that day. Catechism for the children followed at noon with another sermon at 3 P.M. (Apparently there was no NFL football on Sunday afternoons back then!) On the working days, additional sermons came on Monday, Wednesday, and Friday.

The argument of Calvin and the city fathers of Geneva was the same as that of Proverbs 29:18. It warned that "Where there is no vision [the Hebrew word stood for "divine revelation"], the people perish [or, as translated in Exodus 32:25, "the people run wild" or "become ungovernable"]" (KJV). Can we in our day and generation recognize that the very same results come from biblical and theological illiteracy? Surely, there is deep concern about a society that seems to have lost its moorings. Our cities and towns have become more like human jungles in which we devour each other for little or no apparent reason. Only a word from God can save us from the path of self-destruction that we seem to be on.

But how does such a transformed state of affairs come about? The answer is this: It happens just as it did in Samuel's day. It happens when God shows us the first characteristic of his powerful word, or message, namely, God can make that word just as *scarce* for us as he did for those in Samuel's day (v. 1). God can withdraw his teachers from the scene so that the hearing of his Word becomes a rare commodity. And when he does, society seems to come unglued, and all the fury of evil breaks loose. The cohesive bonding of our relationships gives way with such force that we are astounded at how brutish human beings can act. Schools suddenly become just as unsafe as the killing fields of Vietnam. Much of this takes place because we have decided we can make it on our own without God's revelation or his help. Second only to the gift of God's Son was the gift of his Word. But that is all too easily forfeited in life and in the pulpit for some other substitute.

Individuals cannot substitute anything in place of the basic necessity of living by every word that proceeds from the mouth of God. We cannot manipulate that word, manufacture another form of it, or duplicate it. It is unique; it is life-giving. Only the

Lord can give it. Therefore, we say, that word can become scarce and rare in its exposure to people with the result that we, along with previous cultures, witness what we have seen in recent days.

Our Lord can also make that word scarce in its effects on us and our times. Amos 8:11–12 warns of a time when the Lord will send a famine, not of bread and water, but "a famine of hearing the word of God." Therefore, when God grows silent, the darkness thickens, and often the depths of our gloom and sadness become almost unbearable.

The second characteristic of the powerful word of God can be seen in the ways in which God can make that word *startling* to us (vv. 2–14). We can be startled by the way that word calls us, as it did Samuel. Eleven times in verses 4–10, some form of the word "call" appears as our Lord tries to get the attention of young Samuel.

Meanwhile, Eli was losing his physical eyesight, if not, more seriously, his spiritual vision. It was Samuel who was needed to make sure the lamp of God did not go out in the tabernacle. God had providentially provided Samuel through Hannah's earlier agonizing petitions to our heavenly Father.

It took four calls from God to get through to Samuel. Was it that Samuel was a little dull and somewhat dim-witted here? I doubt it, for in explaining his response, verse 7 does not seem to blame Samuel. The point is that such was the state of religious affections at this time that a boy raised in the house of God was ignorant of the person and work of God. Before we castigate those men and their times, consider the state of biblical illiteracy in our day for people who have grown up in the center of our evangelical churches! That is not the case with all, mind you, but it is common enough to sound the same warnings found in this text for our day as well.

But note the kindness and gentleness of the Lord. He does not heap piles of scorn on Samuel; rather, he "stands there" as at other times, calling Samuel. There is no tirade such as, "Boy, you never get anything right." Instead, we see a Savior who is patient, tender, and kind!

Our Lord can make his word startling not only in its call, but also in its content. In fact, so startling were the contents of Samuel's call that it would make the ears of all that heard it tingle. Judgment would visit the house of Eli because he too had failed to act on the word that God had sent to him in 1 Samuel 2:27–29. Eli had done nothing to restrain the wickedness of his two priestly sons. Trivializing the holiness of God is serious business indeed. His sons had literally "blasphemed" the Lord (v. 13 in the Greek version of this Hebrew text). So severe was the sin and guilt that it could never be atoned for by sacrifice or offering!

It is this dual nature of the message that we hear from Scripture that is sometimes troubling. The message both attracts and repels. Dale Ralph Davis's book on this passage has an illustration from Andrew Bonar.[16] The story is about a Grecian artist who painted a picture of a boy carrying a basket of grapes on his head. So glorious was the painting that all demanded that the artist place it on display in the Grecian forum. So graphic and real were the grapes in the basket that the birds flew up to the canvas and tried to peck at the grapes. The citizens of the city heaped volumes of praise on the artist, for they said even the birds were fooled by the depictions represented on the canvas. But the artist declined all their praise, saying, "No, I should have done a great deal more. I should have painted the boy so true to life that the birds would not have dared to come near." He thought it should have been both attractive and repelling at the same time. Therein lies precisely the tension found in the Word of God. To smother people with the comfort of the gospel while never telling them about their sin is lopsided. But to preach angrily and focus only on judgment with no encouragement or care for persons is likewise missing the point of revelation. God's messengers must hold high the truth of God in both its judgment and its comfort. We must afflict the comfortable and comfort the afflicted as teachers and ministers of the gospel.

A third characteristic of the powerful word of God is that it is *sovereign* over us (vv. 15–18). Our Lord is sovereign over the speaker. That sovereignty rules over all, for most speakers have a natural tendency to fear announcing judgment. Clearly, Samuel shared this fear (v. 15), but when Eli called Samuel to learn what God had said, Samuel "told him everything" (v. 18). Why should we hide the word God has spoken, for it is true and it will come to pass whether we are faithful in announcing it or not. In fact, the text suggests that if we as God's messengers hold back the truth, then the guilt that falls on the audience also falls on us for failing to sound the warning so that they would have a chance to change and avoid the threatened calamity.

But God is sovereign over the audience as well. Eli did not reject, argue, or dispute the validity of the message Samuel gave to him. To his credit, he simply said, "He is the LORD" (v. 18). God's people are taught to say "Amen" to the judgments of God as well as to the blessings from above. He is Lord indeed.

The reason is fairly straightforward: If God did not judge evil, then the good and the righteous would be discouraged. God is not a paper tiger who threatens but never carries out his threats. Should the pulpit pull punches, as it were, the moment it did so would be the very moment that God would despise the pulpit and give it no standing before a watching world or even before his church.

The final characteristic of the powerful word of God found in this passage is that God's word *secures* and accredits the servants he sends to us. It is no secret that many pulpit ministries are lightly regarded by both friends and foes alike. That is why even the word *preach* is used in a pejorative way. For example, people say, "Don't preach to me," or "Don't get preachy with me." But there is no need for worrying about such opinions if one is focusing the message on the Word of God.

Nothing spoken from the revelation of God by his servants will fall to the ground (v. 19). It will no more fail in its task than the snow and rain will fail in the task they are sent to do from heaven (Isa. 55:10–11). The question is this: Is our confidence in the Word of God that strong? Do we think that God in his revelation centuries ago will be a match for the crises we face here today? Is it adequate to reach our own young people, the unreached peoples of the earth, or even the modern cynic that feels no one has the right to tell another what is right or wrong, true or false?

Despite all the odds of our day and that day in Israel, everyone knew that Samuel's work and message were accredited by God. This raises the whole question, What really validates our ministries as teachers and preachers of the gospel? Is it growth in the physical plant? Is it growth in the number of attendees? Is it growth in income dollars? Or are we best validated, as this text teaches, by the words taught and the ability those words evidence to effect change in persons' lives to the glory of God?

One thing is for sure: When such authoritative announcements come from the Word of God, its power will be seen by all. A by-product of such effective preaching is that its relevancy and effectiveness will be apparent to all (4:1a).

So what shall we say to all of this? Can the light of revelation shine through the present darkness? And if it can, as we are bound to say, how else can it break out except through the faithful preaching of the Word of God?

The truth is, where there is no vision [i.e., input of the revelation of God], the people go wild (Prov. 29:18). And the price for allowing a famine of the word of God to fester is that an outbreak of evil appears in almost all the other areas of life.

It is high time that teachers and preachers return to the basics once again. Whereas many had thought that the teaching of the Word in a straightforward exposition was now too dated to be effective, it is time to repent and change the menu on the table of the teachings that we spread for the general populace, as well as for the people of God. Let us covenant before God that we will be faithful to the Word of God, longing only to see in evidence the power that Word promises. Let us determine not to cater merely to the current appetites of the pew or join the fashions of the day with what is in vogue as far as proclamation methods are concerned. Instead, let us form a whole new cadre of men and women: "Proclaimer-Keepers" to the glory of God. Only then will a new and unique power be seen in the church as God shows us anew the power of himself in his Word!

6

Preaching and Teaching the Wisdom Books of the Old Testament

Fred Craddock argued some time ago:

> Why should the multitude of forms and moods within the Biblical literature and the multitude of needs in the congregation be brought together in one unvarying [preaching] mold, and that copied from Greek rhetoricians of centuries ago? An unnecessary monotony results, but more profoundly, there is an inner conflict between the content of the sermon and its form.[1]

Indeed, why should it?

And thus it has become necessary to allow the form and genre of the passage of Scripture to shape the form of the message. This is the revolution that has occurred in the field of preaching in the last twenty-five years.

But how far can we take this line of thinking? John Holbert, for example, complained that the Bible was "misused" when the text of Scripture was read in search of themes or points that were distilled from all biblical texts.[2] Instead of looking for a discursive, didactic, or conceptual type of sermon that "makes points," Holbert, as Craddock did in the citation noted above, warned that preachers should move 180 degrees from that type of Hellenistic rhetoric. Holbert, however, was not saying that didactic preaching is no longer effective or even that it is not desirable. His point was that there are important alternatives to the discursive method of preaching.

I have no trouble affirming that there is as wide a breadth of preaching as there are literary types in Scripture. I am not so sure, however, that using all of those various types will in every case lead us away from "making points," or from didactic aspects of the ministry. After all, all Scripture, argued Paul, was given for a number of different purposes (2 Tim. 3:14–17), but all contributes to either introducing us to faith in Christ or building us up and challenging all of us to grow as believers.

The point is that genre-sensitive preaching must be governed by the rhetorical strategies of that genre. Whether this means that "point-making" in sermons will be dropped in favor of some other replacement for sermon outcomes is another matter. That can be investigated later in this chapter.

The Genre of the Proverb

In some ways, proverbs are not all that different from narratives, for in some sense, proverbs arise out of recurring story lines. No wonder, then, that proverbs have been defined as "short sentence[s] founded upon long experience[s], containing a truth."[3] Recurring patterns of stories gave rise to a short sentence that tended to wrap up the truth of the narrative in a memorable phrase or line.

Proverbs abound in all of life, as well as in the Bible. It is the wise person who can recall that sagacious line and link it at the appropriate moment with the new situation that bears such striking similarities with a situation in the past. As such, proverbs have the potential for giving direction, group or individual analyses, and ethical formation in the face of brand-new settings. Proverbs work this way because they condense a lot of wisdom into a rather broad generalization that captures the essence of patterns that tend to repeat themselves. These generalizations come in various shapes, settings, situations, and sizes.

But if all of this is so, why is it that so few sermons go to the wisdom materials as a basis for a word from God? A host of explanations usually arises in answer to this question.

The most obvious is that many expositors find preaching from the Book of Proverbs just plain difficult. There does not appear at first glance to be any order, unity, or structure to the book. How is one to give even the semblance of an expository sermon, which is being held up as the model form in this book, when the material seems to resist such an approach at every point?

Some evangelical expositors will feel especially reluctant to preach from Proverbs because they cannot find the announcement of the gospel in this book. But that must raise another question: Is the sole reason for preaching to bring the good news of salvation in every message? Is it not possible for preaching to address the believer and call for a response in light of the teaching of God's Word on ethics, morals, and an exemplary lifestyle? One need only note how prevalent in our culture today are the issues of dishonesty, marital unfaithfulness, divorce, domestic violence with its resulting physical abuse, drug abuse, unruly children, submission to peer pressure, financial mismanagement, and forms of entrapment in society and the church itself to realize how relevant the proverbs are that cover these issues! These issues cry out for courageous proclamation and biblical instruction.

The case for preaching the wisdom from the Book of Proverbs can be expanded even more. It even goes beyond morals and ethics, for as Brevard Childs has noted:

> The didactic function of biblical wisdom literature is far broader than that which is usually implied by the term ethics. When the sage challenged his pupils to pursue wisdom, it not only involved moral decisions regarding wrong and right behavior, but was an intellectual and pragmatic activity which sought to encompass the totality of experience. Nevertheless, it is striking that the pattern of human conduct, which the sage sought to inculcate, overlapped to a large extent with that set as obedient behavior within the Pentateuch and prescribed for the covenant people.[4]

Some time ago I had made a similar point by noting that so much of the Book of Proverbs was a mere representation in proverbial form of what had been announced in the legal sections of the Torah.[5] Therefore, wisdom is not offered as a substitute for faith or belief; it is offered to teach those who have found faith in the coming seed of promise through the line of

Abraham, Isaac, Jacob, and David about how we are to live the
life of obedience as an evidence of that faith.

Unlike the law of God in the Torah, from which so much of
the Book of Proverbs finds its spiritual source, wisdom expands
on the same themes and instructs how one can put these same
principles into practical and useful application in everyday life.

Its teaching may appear at times to be so "secular" and devoid
of spiritual principles that it merely demands good social graces
and common sense. But we are assured that God is just as interested in what we may relegate to the realm of the mundane and
trivial as he is in the megadecisions and movements of our day.
He must be Lord over all aspects of life and living.

Interpreting Proverbs' Wisdom

If we are to preach on the Book of Proverbs, how shall we
approach this book and interpret it for our day? Surely it stands
on a different plane than Benjamin Franklin's *Poor Richard's
Almanac!* Of course, it presents itself as the Word of God; that
is one of its most distinctive features. But it does share many
other similarities with proverbs in general. Most importantly,
Alyce M. McKenzie shows how biblical proverbs share many
syntactic properties with secular proverbs.[6] She lists five such
properties of proverbs: (1) self-containment, (2) a fixed form,
(3) the use of the present or future tense, (4) an eschewal of first-
person pronouns, and (5) the possession of poetic features.
Rather than being a mere incomplete phrase, proverbs contain
a complete thought. In addition to their usual fixed form, the
most characteristic aspect of a proverb is that it involves a partial generalization arising out of a rather specific situation,
which in turn is applied to parallel a new situation.

It is important to realize that these are not universal truths that
apply equally to all situations. Proverbs also prefer to use the present tense and avoid the use of first-person pronouns and posses-
sives. This quality tends to give a proverb its timeless appearance
and tempts the interpreter to universalize its meaning so that it
fits every situation without exception. But this temptation must
be avoided, lest the preacher become too simplistic and reduc-

tionistic by assuming that the *prima facie* meaning is in every case to be universalized, or that it contains no exceptions. Instead, the proverb intends to cover most cases without claiming that it fits every conceivable instance of things that appear alike. To claim that it does fit everything everywhere is to overextend the genre and to treat it as if it were a form of expositional prose!

The most basic form of a proverb is one that has only one descriptive element, such as, "Money talks," or "Time flies." But more commonly, the proverb exhibits a more complex structure. McKenzie describes that form as consisting of three essential components: (1) the proverb *image*, which is the literal level of the proverb, (2) the proverb *message*, which is the ultimate meaning, or referent of the proverb, and (3) an *architectural formula*, which is the relationship between the topic and the comments made on that topic.[7] These architectural formulas, consisting of topic-comment relationships, assume two basic forms, according to McKenzie: *equational proverbs*, in which the formula is A equals B, and *oppositional proverbs*, in which A does not equal B. These can be illustrated by the following proverbs:

Equational Proverbs:
"Do not love sleep or you will grow poor." (Prov. 20:13)
    The Form: A equals B

"Where your treasure is, there your heart will be also." (Matt. 6:21)
    The Form: Where there is A, there is B

"Where there are no oxen, the manger is empty." (Prov. 14:4)
    The Form: Where there is no A, there is no B

Oppositional Proverbs:
"All a man's ways seem right to him, but the LORD weighs the heart." (Prov. 21:2)
    The Form: A does not equal B

"Better a little with the fear of the LORD than great wealth with turmoil." (Prov. 15:16)
    The Form: Better A than B

"Better is a dinner of vegetables where love is than a fatted ox and hatred with it." (Prov. 15:17 NRSV)
The Form: Better A than B

Besides the common meaning that words have in their communities, Proverbs also exhibits a frequent use of metaphor, metonymy, and simile. For example, a *simile* is a formal comparison (using the words "as" or "like") made between two different objects. Thus, "a beautiful woman who shows no discretion" is *like* "a gold ring in a pig's snout" (Prov. 11:22). Likewise, "*As* a door turns on its hinges, so a sluggard turns on his bed" (Prov. 26:14). Again, "*Like* clouds and wind without rain is a man who boasts of gifts he does not give" (Prov. 25:14). The words "like" or "as" tip the interpreter off to the presence of an expressed comparison (A is like/as B).

A *metaphor*, on the other hand, is an implied or unexpressed comparison. For example, Proverbs 10:15 has "the wealth of the rich is their fortified city." Genesis 49:9 says, "You are a lion's cub, O Judah." And in Luke 13:32 Jesus said of King Herod, "Go tell that fox. . . ." Herod had only one thing in common with the fox: both were sly and crafty!

Another figure of speech is *metonymy*, which means a change of a name or a substitution of a name in order to give a force and an impression not otherwise attainable. In Proverbs, the "lip" and "tongue" are often used to stand for something else. For example, "The *lip* of truth shall be established forever, but only for a moment [literally, "until I shall wink"] the *tongue* of falsehood" (Prov. 12:19, my translation). Consider this: "A gentle *tongue* can break a bone" (Prov. 25:15). In these illustrations, the "lip" or "tongue" stands for what these anatomical parts *produce* or what comes forth from them, rather than the anatomical parts in and of themselves.

Care must be exercised by the teacher or preacher to observe these figures of speech, for not only do they affect the interpretation, but much more interestingly, they also give a certain color and flair to the teaching and preaching that otherwise would not be present.

Moving from the Proverb to the Sermon

The preacher usually is well advised not to use individual proverbs (i.e., one or two liners) as discrete and separate texts in and of themselves, but rather to employ clusters of proverbs that focus on similar topics. There is more connection and contextual relationship between an individual proverb and the ones preceding and following it than has been acknowledged heretofore. This will be basic to our contention that one can teach or preach from textual clusters of proverbs rather than being reduced to treating each proverb in isolation or in a topical fashion only. Recent study in the New Testament Book of James has come to the same conclusion. There is more in each context that binds what otherwise seems to be disparate parts together into units of thought than had previously been realized.

What are the questions that the teacher or preacher needs to ask if he or she is to move from a set of proverbs to a lesson or sermon? In what order should these questions be asked in order to move easily toward a fresh contemporary presentation of the truth found in these wise words?[8]

1. Look first to see if this proverb is part of a proverbial cluster on a particular subject. One example of this type of grouping can be found in Proverbs 11:1–21, as is pointed out by Duane Garrett. Proverbs 11:1–21 forms an *inclusio* with the concepts of what is an abomination to the Lord and what is his delight in verses 1 and 20. The smaller collections that are found between these two bookends, as it were, form subunits of this main theme. Verses 1–4 describe God's abhorrence of fraud (v. 1) and his promise that the wrongfully gained wealth of the wicked will do them no good in the day of judgment (v. 4), while humility and integrity are the best guides (vv. 2, 3).

   A second subtheme within this larger theme of God's abhorring the wicked but delighting in the righteous is found in the couplet of verses 7 and 8. These two verses are bound together by another *inclusio* with "wicked" in the beginning of verse 7 and the end of verse 8. Once again, the hopelessness, misery, and purposelessness of the wicked life is contrasted with the deliverance and hope-filled lives of the righteous.

A third subtheme is found in verses 9–13. Verses 9 and 12 parallel each other in that they treat the destruction of a neighbor through slander, while verses 10–11 make up an obvious parallel couplet.

Verse 13, while outside the *chiasmus*, renders an afterword on the subject of the tongue: Not only are the wicked malicious in the use of their tongues, but they are not discreet; they just cannot be trusted!

There are many other proverb groupings that are often missed by interpreters. Some of the more obvious ones are Proverbs 22:17–24:22 and the different collections in Proverbs 25–31 as indicated in part by their headings.

2. Ask whether there are any literary connections between the proverb under investigation and the text that precedes or follows it. This is similar to the previous question, but it dramatizes the need to study the context more forcefully. For instance, one may land on Proverbs 6:27–28 as the desired text for teaching or preaching: "Can a man scoop fire into his lap without his clothes being burned? Can a man walk on hot coals without his feet being scorched?" But the context of these two verses is Proverbs 6:20–35. It is in the context of a warning against adultery that these metaphorical questions are raised in verses 27 and 28. The student is being warned to stay away from the immoral woman (v. 24), for the one who "sleeps with another man's wife" will not "go unpunished" (v. 29).

In the same way, one may randomly choose Proverbs 19:20–21 as a text, but it could prove to be reductionistic or wrongly interpreted if one does not recognize that the context for these verses is actually Proverbs 19:16–23. Garrett finds that these eight verses revolve around the theme of the disciplined and prudent life. At the beginning and end of these verses on the good life are the twin themes of keeping God's commandments (v. 16) and living in reverence for him (v. 23). The structure would look like this according to Garrett:[9]

A: Adherence to God's way is life (v. 16)
  B: Give to the poor (v. 17)
    C: Discipline your son (Hebrew: *ns'*, v. 18)
    C': Allow the intemperate to pay the price
      (Hebrew: *ns'*, v. 19)
      D: Submit to instruction (Hebrew: *'sh*, v. 20)
      D': Acknowledge Providence (Hebrew: *'sh*,
        v. 21)
  B': Better poor but honest (v. 22)
A': Fear of Yahweh is life (v. 23)

3. Ask what individual strophes, subunits, or parallel constructions make up the larger grouping or united topic of the collected proverbs. Just as one must determine the main theme or topic sentence of every paragraph in a prose genre or the major idea of every scene in a narrative genre, so here one must see how each smaller grouping of individual proverbs contributes to the theme of the collection or larger group in this chapter or part of a chapter. When these minor groupings have been identified, then one must ask how each contributes to the total subject in which they are embraced. The example from Proverbs 6 can serve as an illustration here again. Thus, the sixth exhortation (of seven exhortations in Prov. 1:8–9:18) deals with the topic of adultery (Prov. 6:20–35). Typically, the exhortation begins with an appeal for the son to heed his father's words (vv. 20–23). Verses 24–26 plainly state that the immoral woman is alluring, beautiful, and captivating, but she is also deadly in moral terms. Then come the metaphorical questions about handling fire in one's lap and walking on hot coals in verses 27 and 28, with the point finally being stated in verse 29: that is what sleeping with another man's wife is like! Finally, verses 30–35 show that while there might be some saving of face for the thief who is caught (because of what impelled him to steal), there is only a harsh judgment from an outraged husband, who will rain fury on the head of the adulterer and will refuse to be assuaged by any sort of compensation. Thus there are four subgroups of this one exhortation in verses 20–35, which can make up the four main points of a sermon or lesson.

4. What are the theological norms and informing doctrines announced in earlier Scriptures that are now encapsulated in this new proverbial grouping that forms the basis for our lesson or sermon? Proverbs teaches that all of human life is lived in the context of a sovereign God who has showed us how we ought to live. There is a pattern or order that comes as a gift from God for all of life and for all of its relationships.

Nonproverbial Wisdom

Wisdom materials appear throughout the Old Testament. Aside from those places where entire books are dedicated to a wisdom-type genre, there appear instances of nonproverbial wisdom embedded in other genres. One need only think of the riddle of Samson in Judges 14:14 ("Out of the eater, something to eat; out of the strong, something sweet") or the fables told by Jehoash, king of Israel, in 2 Kings 14:9 and Jotham in Judges 9:7–15 (the only two fables in the Bible). But there are three Old Testament books in which there is a mixture of genres that call for special attention.

Ecclesiastes

Many have found the wisdom displayed in the Book of Ecclesiastes to be particularly difficult because it seems so speculative, pessimistic, and counter to what one would expect in the canon of the Old Testament. Indeed, Ecclesiastes is a blend of wisdom forms, for one can identify allegory (on old age in 12:1–7), example-story (9:13–16), proverbs (7:1–29), and more.

But, as the epilogue of Ecclesiastes 12:9–14 will demonstrate, it would be a mistake to regard this book as a loose collection of contradictory and polarized statements. The only way to uphold that negative thesis is to argue that the final two verses of the book were added later on in order to sanitize the book and make it possible to adopt it into the canon. The problem with that view is that no existing complete manuscript of Ecclesiastes is without this ending and no evidence exists to demonstrate that an authoritative body decided this book (or any other) was indeed "canonical" or by such a means "legitimated"! Thus, once the epilogue is adopted as an original part of the book, that argument evaporates.

This book has a clear and consistent plan. Its divisions are easily detected by the repeated rhetorical device that advises, "Eat, drink and realize the benefit of one's labor" (Eccles. 2:24; 5:18; and 8:15, my translation), thereby giving the book four clearly demarcated sections to its argument. These divisions and the argument go as follows:

1. Life is a gift from God (1:2–2:26)
2. God has an all-encompassing plan (3:1–5:20)
3. This plan must be explained and applied (6:1–8:15)
4. Discouragements must be removed for believers who apply this plan of God (8:16–12:7)[10]

Job

Here is another book that is a mixture or blend of several genres. Along with hymns (e.g., Job 28), proverbs (e.g., 5:17), and riddles (e.g., 41:1–5), the book has a heavy emphasis on dialogue and disputation. In the midst of these long exchanges between Job and his so-called comforters are lawsuit genres (23:1–7), soliloquy (chap. 31), and the use of a large number of such figures of speech as irony (12:2), simile (14:2), metaphor (16:13), and metonymy (16:19).

Job, then, is not easily classified in a single genre classification. Nor does it have a literary parallel in ancient Near Eastern wisdom literature. It is a *sui generis*—its own unique type of literature.

One must teach or preach on Job in its dialogical form, which sets up the questions from the speeches of the three so-called friends and finds their response from a revelational point of view in the counterarguments given by Job. God stated his estimate of the sayings of Job's three friends when he concluded: "I am angry with you [Eliphaz] and your two friends [Bildad and Zophar], because you have not spoken of me what is right, as my servant Job has" (Job 42:7b). Thus, while suffering plays a large part in the book, it is not Job who is on trial but God! The teacher and preacher must be careful, therefore, *not* to make the speeches of Job's so-called friends normative, for in Job 42:7 God declares that their speeches were incorrect and, as a consequence, not revelational!

Song of Solomon

Canticles, or the Song of Songs, as this book is also known, has likewise proven to be a conundrum for many teachers of the Word of God. It is best to interpret the book as a song dedicated to the gift of marital love as intended by God, since no clues exist in the book to suggest that the book is to be taken allegorically. Therefore, what the incarnate Word (Jesus himself) did for marriage by attending the marriage feast of Cana, so the written Word (the Bible) has done by giving to us this book.

Of course, the expression "Song of Songs" is the Hebrew way of expressing the superlative form; hence this is the very best song God could give us on this topic of the delights of genuine marital love.

The hermeneutical clue for this book can be found in the similar terms used in the allegory found in Proverbs 5:15–23, as we will demonstrate later in this chapter. The somewhat graphic metaphors used for the couple and the marital act of love should not detract from the seriousness of the topic on which divine revelation must have a part.

The book actually has *three* main characters, not just two. There is Solomon, the maiden, and the shepherd boy from the maiden's hometown. While the Shulamite maiden is somewhat abruptly hauled away to Jerusalem to prepare to join Solomon's harem, she continues to long for the shepherd to whom she was pledged back home. Eventually she is reunited with the shepherd, and the whole point of the book becomes evident in Song of Songs 8:6–7.

> Place me like a seal over your heart,
>   like a seal on your arm;
> for love is as strong as death,
>   its jealousy unyielding as the grave.
> It burns like blazing fire,
>   like a [flame from Yah(weh)].[11]

> Many waters cannot quench love;
> rivers cannot wash it away.
> If one were to give
> all the wealth of his house for love,
> it would be utterly scorned.

It is from this perspective that the book should be taught and preached. Love that God intended for marriage is not something that can be purchased or wooed away by all sorts of tricks or promises of personal position or wealth; it is a gift from God that is to be treasured and used exclusively within the boundaries of marriage!

An Illustration of Preaching from Wisdom: Proverbs 5:15–23

Most interpreters properly describe Proverbs 5:15–23 as an allegory.[12] The reason they do so is because of the extensive use of words or concepts taken from one realm of thought, such as nature, in order to portray concepts that belong to another sphere of thought. An allegory is an extension of a series of metaphors that are united into a single concept and presented from a unified point of view.

But what really tips the hand of the author is the fact that verse 18 suddenly interjects, "May you rejoice in the wife of your youth." After using five water metaphors, this sudden reversion to a direct form of stating things shows that the writer wanted his references to drinking water from one's own well to be understood as having sexual intercourse only with one's own wife. The following preaching or teaching outline develops this theme:

  I. Our spouse is to be our source of enjoyment (v. 15)
 II. Our spouse's relationship must be protected (vv. 16–17)
III. Our delight is in our spouse (vv. 18–20)
 IV. Our relationship with our spouse is exposed to the gaze of God (vv. 21–23)

From this section we can gain not only a key teaching text on marital relations, but also a powerful clue for interpreting the

Song of Solomon. One need only compare Song of Solomon 4:12; 6:2–3, and similar passages to see the striking comparisons. Even more importantly, Proverbs 5:15–23 is more than relevant for today's world as it helps us to take a stand on marital fidelity. Let us see how the text still speaks dramatically to us in our day on the same issues that confronted people in the days of Solomon.

Few times in history have we seen a more open attack on the Bible's code of sexual conduct than in our day. The secular community often has accused Christians of being against sex. It openly mocks Christians' insistence that sexual relationships be confined to marriage as being an antique view that smacks of being puritanical.

Even within the church, many have openly begun to forsake God's way for the new standards of this generation. Rather than being solely a teenage problem, this is increasingly a problem for adults in their middle and senior years, as many choose infidelity and unchastity as a way of life.

Proverbs 5:15–23 describes the end results of such liaisons outside of marriage. But rather than advocating a prudish view of sex, as some accuse Christians and the Bible of advocating, it celebrates the joy of human sexuality, but within a marriage commitment. No one can charge Proverbs 5:15–23 of being against sex. Instead, it reflects the fact that our sexuality is a gift from God and that is what makes it so sublime and its endearments so enjoyable.

To declare all such biblical standards as medieval because we now have antibiotics and various forms of the "pill" is to put science in place of God as the new Savior. Not all violations of God's law are easily handled by science, for the presence of AIDS has given new reasons (I refer only and specifically to those cases of AIDS and HIV that are connected with sexual promiscuity) for pausing to consider the truthfulness of the Scriptures.

True, Alvin Toffler had predicted in his 1970 book *Future Shock* that future marriages would allow for discardable husbands and wives after one or the other had "outgrown" the spouse to whom he or she was pledged. Charles A. Reich in his much heralded book *The Greening of America* claimed in a similar way that young people did not want all the entangling relationships that marriage brings. They just wanted to be free to love as, when, and whom they pleased. Whether this was real freedom, or mere exploitation, became evident in the two decades that followed: It turned out to be exploitation to the extreme.

However, in contrast to these emerging philosophies of exploitation and experimentation, God's purpose for marriage remained the same in Genesis 2:18, "It is not good for the man to be alone." Instead, the two, man and woman, were to be "one flesh."

The first of four reminders is found in Proverbs 5:15, and it is this: Our spouse is to be the source of our enjoyment. The singular nouns, "cistern" and "well," are used here as symbols for the wife. Both are supplies of drinking water and deep satisfaction and refreshment. The enjoyment meant here is not spiritual alone, but sensual, without any attempt to make comparisons to the female form or anatomy. The figure is one of enjoyment and attachment. It is one's *own* well and cistern that provides the refreshment. Thus, the metaphor commands us to be faithful to our spouses. Every clandestine affair or unnatural attraction violates God's clearest injunction. God's original and permanent design is for each one of us to have *one* fountain (the singular form of the nouns is all the more startling in the face of some of the unapproved polygamy that was found in Old Testament times). As Song of Solomon 4:12 says, "You are a garden locked up, my sister, my bride; you are a spring enclosed, a sealed fountain." Likewise, Song of Solomon 4:15 says, "You are a garden fountain, a well of flowing water."

The second reminder is just as straightforward: Our spouse's relationship must be protected (Prov. 5:16–17). We are struck immediately by the switch from the singular nouns of verse 15 to the plural references to "springs" and "streams of water." Here the picture is one of waste, a dispersal of precious water (hence one's sexuality) into the streets and public squares.

The domestic tranquility of the home has somehow been destroyed, for the wife has now gone searching for extramarital affairs, thereby splashing her precious wares all over town. The figure is not of the male, as some have suggested, with the water representing male sperm that have begotten children all over town. Nor is it one of a well that has dried up from lack of use and thus has gone to waste because of her husband's neglect and lack of sensitivity. What settles the question is that in verse 17 the water sources of verses 15, 16, and 18 are said to be "yours alone," that is, the husband's, with the plural nouns still referring to the wife of verse 15.

The third reminder follows: Our delight must be in our spouse (vv. 18–20). The fountain is blessed when she is enjoyed as God intended—that is, within the bonds of marriage. In the Greek Septuagint verse 18 reads: "Let your fountain be for yourself alone."

God's Word commends infatuation with and enthusiastic enjoyment of one's spouse as his gift and design for couples. There is a divinely ordained attraction for the opposite sex, but if it is misused, it leads to destruction (Prov. 7). But within the monogamous state, it is more delightful than wine (Song of Sol. 1:2). It is a flame from the Lord (Song of Sol. 8:6). Therefore, let us "Rejoice in the wife of [our] youth" (Prov. 5:18), for our text likens her to "a loving doe, a graceful [or charming] deer" (v. 19). These animals are used as comparisons here, for they speak of grace, form, and agility of movement, just as Song of Solomon does in 4:5 and 7:3.

There is satisfaction that is to be derived from the sensual and physical aspects of marital lovemaking. More than that, it is viewed as an intoxication in Proverbs 5:19–20. The verb translated "to be captivated" also meant more literally "to be intoxicated." This is how satisfying and enjoyable the pleasures of physical sex are for those who use their sexual gifts as they were divinely intended within marriage.

Finally, we have one last reminder: Our relationship with our spouse is exposed to the gaze of God (vv. 21–23). To the previous arguments for marital fidelity are added two more reasons to be faithful to one's mate. First, God observes everything that happens on planet earth. There never has been a secret rendezvous that escaped God's notice (v. 21). All of our ways are examined, pondered, and weighed so that we might be judged fairly (v. 21b). Thus, we see the reason for the rhetorical question of verse 20, "Why be captivated, my son, by an adulteress?" The God who has given human sexuality has the right to expect a righteous use of this gift. To say it even more bluntly: There is not a motel or lover's lane where God cannot see and know what is happening!

The second reason for being faithful to one's spouse is found in verses 22–23. The husband who chooses to live promiscuously will eventually find himself bound, trapped, and tied up in cords of his own sins. Not only will this lack of discipline result in slavery to his own corrupt self, it will also wreck his marriage and bring about his own death. This is the height of folly (v. 23). The pleasure he sought will evaporate and mock him as the final irony of it all.

Any conclusion that does not see the terrific impact that a text like this could have on our contemporary culture is blind. Clearly, dead marriages are nonbiblical marriages; they do not honor God. Couples must fiercely fight for a daily renewal and growth in their marriage. God has decreed that there must be joy, satisfaction, exclusivity, attentiveness, mystery, beauty, power, and consciousness of the presence of God. His gaze extends even into the bedroom where the marriage act takes place. Sex in marriage is not sordid, worldly, sinful, or mundane for him. It is one of his most beautiful gifts to mortals who follow him; indeed, it is a "song of songs," the best of all songs! By his grace, may we resist the flow of the culture of our day and renew our vows of holy matrimony to the glory of God.

Conclusion

For too long now, the wisdom materials have been forsaken in the preaching mission of the church. People long for help with the basic and mundane issues of life, and preaching on each of the wisdom books can supply their hunger beyond their wildest imaginations. Especially relevant are the texts from Proverbs and those from the Song of Solomon. If the church does not respond once again to this call for help in these areas, we can only hope that in the gracious providence of God parachurch ministries will fill in the gap with offerings such as marriage enrichment seminars and Basic Youth Conflicts sessions. Let us take up the Word of God and preach the whole counsel of God to a waiting and hungry generation!

7

Preaching and Teaching the Prophets of the Old Testament

Christians have usually found it easier to read and apply the messages of the prophets than any other section of the Old Testament, with the possible exceptions of the Psalms and the Book of Genesis. But that is not to say that all that the prophets had to say is transparent and equally easy to preach. Moses was told in Numbers 12:6–8 that "When a prophet of the LORD is among you, I reveal myself to him in visions, I speak to him in dreams. But this is not true of my servant Moses; he is faithful in all my house. With him I speak face to face, clearly and not in riddles." So there is something enigmatic (or like "riddles") about preaching and teaching from the prophets (or at least parts of the prophetic messages) as compared to doing the same thing from the Torah.

Especially difficult are their messages of judgment and words of threatening. Constantly they warned God's people of the judgment that hung over them should they fail to repent and turn from the wicked course they had set their minds to following. Therefore the prophets used every literary device they could imagine to capture the attention and wills of their audiences.[1]

But even if they spoke to their own day with such startling vividness, we must face another question: How are we to hear the word of God today from their texts? If the prophets did speak out so directly on the issues of their times, as most will affirm, then in what way are their messages authoritative and therefore relevant for us today?

It is tempting for some to be dismissive by pointing to
Hebrews 1:1–2a, which says: "In the past God spoke to our fore-
fathers through the prophets at many times and in various ways,
but in these last days he has spoken to us by his Son." The incorrect point that some derive from these New Testament verses is
that the person of Jesus has now replaced the somewhat incomplete words formerly given as a revelation from God by the
prophets. But that is not only an unfair reading of Hebrews
1:1–2a; it also fails to account for the fact that both the first-century church and later Christian generations continued to preserve and use the Old Testament prophets as more than historical curiosities. Or to put the question as William L. Holladay
so graphically phrased it,

> Does God communicate to us through these old words, and if so,
> how are we to hear that communication? Can we untie the boat
> marked "Isaiah" from its moorings in the eighth century b.c. and
> take it down the lake to a mooring in the twentieth [or the twenty-
> first] century a.d. and still recognize it as "Isaiah"? How might
> this be done?[2]

That is precisely what this chapter will attempt to do. Since it
is the same Lord who addresses our generation from the same
standard of holiness and righteousness, it should not be too difficult to hear in the prophets' warnings and insistent calls for
change, repentance, and turning back to God a message for us—
despite the distance in time.

Analyzing the Prophets' Words of Judgment

If we are to hear the words of the prophets in a way that is
both faithful to their original context and of contemporary usefulness to us, we must first determine the basic theme or purpose of each prophetic book from which we wish to preach. It
will also be helpful to show how the purpose of the book fits in
with the overall unifying theme of the whole Old Testament and
the theme or central plan of the whole Bible.

After we have stated the book's purpose, we must then mark
out the major literary sections that constitute the structure of

the book. Usually there are rhetorical devices that mark where a new section begins in the book. However, when such rhetorical devices are not present, one must watch for other markers. A change in subject matter, a change in pronouns, or a change in aspects of the verbal action can all be telltale signs that a new section has begun.

For example, the second half of the Book of Isaiah exhibits three major sections, each with the same colophon (or "tailpiece"): "'There is no peace,' says the LORD, 'for the wicked'" (Isa. 48:22; cf. 57:21). An expansion of that same theme forms the colophon in Isaiah 66:24. Thus, the last part of Isaiah breaks down into three major sections (or enneads, i.e., sets of nine chapters each) as determined by this repeated rhetorical device:

I. The Incomparability of God the *Father* in Isaiah 40–48
"There is no peace . . . for the wicked" (Isa. 48:22).
II. The Atonement of God the *Son* in Isaiah 49–57
"There is no peace . . . for the wicked" (Isa. 57:21).
III. The Work of God the *Holy Spirit* in Isaiah 58–66
"Their worm will not die, nor will their fire be quenched" (Isa. 66:24).

In a similar manner, the prophets Micah and Amos illustrate the use of repeated rhetorical devices to set off the sections of their prophecies. Instead of using a colophon, these two prophets have used "rubrics," or headings, to set off the sections of their books.

"Hear" or "listen," advises Micah in 1:2; 3:1; and 6:1. Accordingly, his book has three major sections to it: Micah 1–2; 3–5; and 6–7.

Amos uses a much more complex rubric. In chapters 1 and 2, eight times he begins, "For three sins of . . . even for four." These headings unify the first section of his book as a set of prophecies addressed to the nations. In his next section, he repeats a phrase that reminds Israel of the great Shema: "Hear this word" (Amos 3:1; 4:1; 5:1). The next section changes its headings to "Woe to you" (Amos 5:18; 6:1). Finally, the book ends with five visions, each beginning with "This is what the Sovereign LORD showed me" (Amos 7:1, 4, 7; 8:1; 9:1 [9:1 uses a variation of the theme to climax the series]). Thus, the book has these four sections: Amos 1–2; 3:1–5:17; 5:18–6:14; 7–9.

Such rhetorical devices are of great assistance to the teacher and preacher in determining the places where the text has a seam indicating another section in the argument of the book.

A third step calls for us to assess the particular genre that was used for a specific message of the prophet. This study is important, for in everyday life, the same words used in different contexts can mean different things depending on whether those words appear in an advertisement, a sermon, or a novel. Therefore, we must investigate the genre, or literary form, used by the prophet and note how it functions in order to both grasp its message and secure an idea as to how we might apply it in our day, age, and culture.

A fourth step that is normally followed at this point is an investigation of the historical and social setting of the book. This helps to focus the work of the interpreter so that the words are heard and understood in the same way that the original audience heard and understood them. However, it runs a risk at the same time. One can pay so much attention to the historical and social contexts (i.e., the things [*res*] pointed to in the text) that the message (*verba*) of the text itself, along with its import for later generations, is never heard in all of its own right. Put another way, sometimes our search for the *Sitz im Leben*, or "setting in life," overpowers the *Sitz im Literatur*, "literary setting." Often the interpreter feels that the task of exegeting the text has been accomplished when the historical, isogogical (i.e., issues of biblical introduction such as date, author, audience, and the like), and apologetical questions (concerning ethical, philosophical, archaeological, or theological matters) have been handled.

Typically, a conservative will treat Joshua 6 by showing that the walls of Jericho did, as a matter of fact, fall away from the city, rather than cave inward toward the city, during the period that belongs to Joshua. This is a good subject for archaeology and apologetics to address, and it is an important subject. But this is not the same thing as treating the message of the text or its claims. Apologetics, in this instance, has swallowed up and usurped the interests of biblical exegesis and properly preparing a passage for preaching.

Now let us return to the third step mentioned above, the identification of genre, for this step will start us off on the right foot for an authentic listening to the text. Each genre will also have its own corresponding sermonic form. Let us see how these literary forms came into existence.

The sixteen writing prophets (the four Major Prophets and the twelve Minor Prophets) built on the precedents that the earlier prophets, such as Samuel, Nathan, Elijah, and Elisha, set for them. For example, it was not uncommon for these earlier prophets (found in the four books of the Earlier Prophets: Joshua, Judges, Samuel, and Kings) to boldly intrude on the royal court's throne room to declare a message from God. Accordingly, the latter prophets (Isaiah, Jeremiah, Ezekiel, Daniel, and the twelve Minor Prophets) assumed a similar role of bursting into the royal palace, acting as messengers or ambassadors from God.[3] From this experience arose a formal manner of presentation that such social settings demanded: the speeches of ambassadors.

Typical of such ambassadorial speeches were the following components, whether they were delivered orally or (later) committed to writing. The two main parts they included were: (1) the sending of the king's exact words, either an accusation or an announcement; and (2) the messenger/ambassador's explanation of those words. One must add to this the fact that in written forms, the messenger would introduce his report by declaring his commission as a messenger of the great king/suzerain, or in the case of the prophets, as one commissioned from God. For example, 1 Kings 21:17 says, "Then the word of the LORD came to Elijah the Tishbite." This will be referred to as the *commission* of the prophet.

That was normally followed by *the messenger formula:* "Thus says the LORD." This formula functioned as the link and means by which the commission and the accusation or announcement were joined. Often a second accusation or an announcement of judgment was added to the first with a second messenger formula.

The reason for such forms of speech was that the king and people had violated the law of God and stood under the prospect of judgment if no evident changes were seen. The announcement of judgment often was not more than one awful, but memorable, sentence. All of these parts need to be illustrated by what follows, lest we dabble in generalities.

An Illustration of a Prophecy of Judgment: Jeremiah 44

Jeremiah 44:1–6

  I. Introduction
   A. The commission: "This word came to Jeremiah concerning all the Jews living in Lower Egypt" (v. 1).
   B. The messenger speech: "This is what the Lord Almighty, the God of Israel, says" (v. 2).
 II. Body
   A. An indication of the situation: "You saw the great disaster I brought on Jerusalem and on all the towns of Judah. Today they lie deserted and in ruins because of the evil they have done. They provoked me to anger by burning incense and worshiping other gods" (vv. 2b–5).
   B. The development of the situation: "Again and again I sent my servants the prophets, who said, 'Do not do this detestable thing that I hate!' But . . . they did not turn from their wickedness or stop burning incense to other gods" (vv. 4–5).
   C. The judgment citation (often beginning with a "therefore"): "Therefore, my fierce anger was poured out . . . and made them the desolate ruins they are today" (v. 6).

Jeremiah 44:7–30

  I. Introduction (of a new declaration [or a continuation of the previous one in vv. 1–6])
   A. The commission: [Missing, or presumed carried on from v. 1]
   B. The messenger speech: "Now this is what the Lord God Almighty, the God of Israel, says" (v. 7).
 II. Body
   A. An indication of the situation, introduced by two interrogatives: "Why bring such great disaster on yourselves by cutting off from Judah the men and women, the children and infants, and so leave yourselves without a remnant? Why provoke me to anger with what your

hands have made, burning incense to other gods in Egypt, where you have come to live?" (vv. 7b–8a).

B. The development of the situation: You are destroying yourselves. You have forgotten the wickedness done by your fathers, kings, and queens of Judah. To this day, you have not humbled yourselves, shown reverence, or followed the law I set before you and your fathers (vv. 8b–10, paraphrased).

C. The prediction of disaster (introduced once again by "therefore"): "Therefore, this is what the LORD Almighty, the God of Israel, says" (v. 11a).

D. The judgment citation: "I am determined to bring disaster on you and to destroy all Judah" (v. 11b). The remnant will perish in Egypt. They will all become an object of horror and cursing. I will punish them in Egypt with sword, famine, and plague as I punished Jerusalem. None of the remnant who have gone to Egypt will escape or survive (vv. 12–14, paraphrased).

III. Concluding responses: The men, who knew what their wives had done, said, "We will not listen to the message you have spoken to us in the name of the LORD!" (v. 17). Before revival came [under King Josiah] we were well off and we had plenty of everything, but ever since we stopped burning incense to the Queen of Heaven, we have had nothing, and we are perishing (vv. 17b–18, paraphrased). Jeremiah responded, "Go ahead then, do what you promised [to Asherah]! Keep your vows!" (v. 25b). But the Lord says let us just wait and see "whose word will stand—mine or [yours]?" (v. 28b).

Such were the prophecies of judgment. With the use of this genre, we are prepared to form the points of our sermon or lesson. This judgment form is often contrasted with the oracles or prophecies of salvation, which we will now consider.

Analyzing Prophecies of Salvation

The common thread that ties the Old and New Testaments together is the single theme of the promise of God.[4] This thread of promise is known by a host of other terms, such as *blessing*, the *contents* of the numerous covenants in the Bible, or the redemptive *history of God's salvation*. Regardless of the terms, the emphasis is on the goodness and grace of God that picks up sinners who are unable to help themselves.

The New Testament, in reflecting on the main message of the Old Testament, uses the word "promise" (Greek, *epangelia*) to depict all that the Savior has done for a lost humanity. The full force of this line of the promise-plan of God began in Genesis 3:15 and 9:27, but it came into full bloom in the oft-repeated promises given to the patriarchs, Abraham, Isaac, and Jacob.

These words of promised salvation are continued in the prophetic oracles of salvation. The only difference between those earlier promises and the prophetic messages of salvation and promise is the context for the prophets' word from God. They usually came in the midst of a threat of judgment for Israel's breach of the covenant, her idolatry, and her sin. Since the promise had been made only by God and was part of a unilateral covenant in which mortals did not obligate themselves as a requirement for the benefits of salvation, the sin of Israel could not derail God's plan to bless Israel and the nations (Judg. 2:1; Jer. 5:18).

The appearance of these words of promise and blessing seem so out of place in the contexts of judgment messages that scholars have often decided the message originally was either one of judgment or one of blessing; it could not have been both. But indeed both were true parts of the tradition.

An Illustration of a Prophecy of Salvation: Jeremiah 32:36–44

The prophetic words of salvation exhibit many of the same constituent parts as the prophecies of judgment.[5] These prophecies could appear in a historical narrative or in the prophetic writings themselves, but the features were pretty much the same. There was the messenger formula to begin with. It would begin, "Thus says the LORD," or "This is what the LORD, the God of Israel, says."

Then came the words addressed either to individuals (as was usually the case in the days of the Earlier Prophets in the books of Joshua, Judges, Samuel, and Kings) or to groups of people. These were the oracles of salvation, or words of encouragement that despite human failure God would intervene, usually at the slightest sign of repentance and turning back to him.

These oracles of salvation fell into two main groups: promises of salvation and proclamations of salvation. Each traditionally had three components: (1) a reassurance that God's promise was still true, (2) the basis for this reassurance, and (3) the future transformation of judgment into salvation and blessing.

Few formal parallels to these oracles of salvation can be found in other literature of the ancient Near East. Certain stereotypical formulas can be attested, such as "Fear not!" or "[The temples] or [the rains] will be restored to you," but that is not the same thing as the genre discussed here.

An example of a salvation prophecy can be seen in the rich chapter of Jeremiah 32, especially verses 36–44. The outline of the genre would look like this:

I. The Messenger Formula: "This is what the LORD, the God of Israel, says" (v. 36c).
II. The Reassurance: "I am the LORD, the God of all mankind. Is anything too hard for me?" (v. 27; see also v. 17).
III. The Future Transformation
   A. "I will surely gather them from all the lands where I banish them in my furious anger and great wrath" (v. 37a).
   B. "I will bring them back to this place and let them live in safety" (v. 37b).
   C. "They will be my people, and I will be their God" (v. 38).
   D. "I will give them singleness of heart and action, so that they will always fear me for their own good and the good of their children after them" (v. 39).
   E. "I will make an everlasting covenant with them: I will never stop doing good to them" (v. 40a).
   F. "I will rejoice in doing them good and will assuredly plant them in this land with all my heart and soul" (v. 41).
IV. The Reassurance: "I will restore their fortunes" (v. 44b).

In interpreting promises of salvation, one must be careful to relate these new assurances, which came in the context of some of the nation's worst tragedies, to the revelation of God's previous promises found in the earlier texts of Scripture. They are all part and parcel of one ongoing "promise" of God. They are based on God's previous word, and they complement it as well.

Other Prophetic Genres

Besides the judgment and salvation messages, there are a number of other literary genres that the prophets used. These may be mentioned briefly since they are subsets of the two main types.

The Woe Oracles

These messages begin with an exclamatory word of dismay, using the word "Woe!" or "Alas!" (Hebrew: *hoy*). This exclamation is then usually followed by a participle that describes the action that is being cited as offensive to God, or it is followed by a noun that characterizes the people in a negative way. Some believe that the social setting for these words was the cries of despair lifted up at a funeral. Regardless of what walk of life the forms/genres originated in, the prophets cried out in a message of despair over the belligerency of the people.

Such clusters of woe burden messages can be found in Isaiah 5; 10:1–11; 28:1–4; 29:1–4, 15; 30:1–3; 31:1–4; Amos 5:18–6:7; Micah 2:1–4; and Habakkuk 2:6–19.

The Prophetic Lawsuit (rib)

In this genre, Yahweh summons Israel or Judah to appear in court to hear the case that has been gathered against them. The parts of this lawsuit are as follows: (1) An appeal for the jury to listen closely (a jury usually made up of the heavens and the earth), (2) the questioning of the witnesses and a statement of the accusation, (3) the prosecution's address to the court, usually contrasting God's salvific acts of grace with the people's sin, and (4) a call to turn back and to obey God. This form reflects, in large part, many of the features of international treaty forms of that day. The best illustration of this type of genre is Micah 6:1–8. The case is just as dramatic in Isaiah 41, where a council is convened among all the peoples on earth and witnesses are summoned as God sets forth his case in verses 21–29. During this trial the sudden announcement of God's summoning a man from the east, later to be known as King Cyrus, becomes the central surprise of the trial.

The Oracles against Foreign Nations

In the Major Prophets alone, over 25 chapters and 680 verses (a bulk of material that exceeds all the chapters and verses in all of the apostle Paul's prison epistles!) are given over to this one literary form (Isa. 13–23; Jer. 46–51; Ezek. 25–32). One could also add Amos 1–2, and the entire Books of Nahum and Obadiah.

The setting within the book for each of these blocks of material is most interesting. For example, the section in Isaiah 13–23 has as bookends prophecies of the first advent of Messiah in Isaiah 7–12 and prophecies of the second advent of Messiah in Isaiah 24–27. Surely this is of significance to the interpreter just as much as the forms of the text are.

The messages to these nations embrace all of the above forms used by the prophets. But their setting, in each book, carries unique force as seen in the Isaiah example.

Guidelines for Interpreting the Prophets

Too often the prophets are thought of mainly as predictors of the future. But the truth is that they were mainly *forthtellers,* for they spoke forth the word of God over against the rising tide of idolatry, apostasy, and sin of the nation. The forthtelling types of messages occupy well over two-thirds of their books; only one-third is devoted to any type of prediction of the future— foretelling.

But in that regard, some care must be taken to distinguish between the prophetic words that were unconditional and unilateral versus those prophecies that were conditioned on the responses of the person(s) addressed. The unconditional promises of God were those of the Abrahamic, Davidic, and new covenants, wherein God alone obligated himself to fulfill what he had said. Parallel to these unconditional promises found in the main covenants were those like the covenant with the seasons in Genesis 8 and the promise of the new heavens and the new earth in Isaiah 65 and 66. Nothing in these promises was contingent on the obedience of mortals; God alone would see to their completion. Not everyone would participate in these blessings, however. Even some in the Davidic family merely transmitted these benefits to the next generation in the line of Messiah and did not participate in them, because they did not receive them by faith.

But all other words of declared judgment had an expressed or unexpressed contingency clause in their words of certain doom. The best illustration of this is in the story of Jonah. While he gave a confident message that in forty days judgment would descend on Nineveh, he had the awful feeling that if the Assyrians ever repented, then God would relent, and the judgment would be stayed for a period of time. Much to the chagrin of the prophet, that is exactly what took place. More than a century later, the same nation, in another generation, felt that the prophet Jonah had falsely cried "wolf" and that their relatives had repented when there was no need to do so. Therefore, they did not repent, and the judgment Jonah would have loved to see finally came upon them.

The principle for this assertion about interpreting the prophets can be found in Jeremiah 18:7–10. In that text, God clearly announced this very principle. Its provisions were as follows: Whenever the Lord announces that a nation is to be destroyed, and that nation repents, then God will not bring the disaster he had threatened them with, despite the fact that there were no contingency clauses, no "ifs" and "unlesses" directly listed with the threat. However, just as true was the reverse situation: God may declare his blessing on a nation only to find that nation cares very little, if at all, for him. God will then rescind his word of promise to bless that people by bringing disaster on that nation he would have blessed had they responded differently.

The messages about the Messiah in the prophets are just as dependable as the other messages of promise and salvation. They too belong to a long, ongoing tradition of the seed promised in the various covenants. They are oracles of salvation with a redemptive history as their heritage. This is not to say that the Messiah may be found behind every proverbial bush in the Old Testament, much less in the prophecies of judgment against the foreign nations. But it cannot be denied that the heart of the promise-plan of God is christocentric without being christoexclusivistic.

An Illustration of Prophetic Preaching: Isaiah 40:12–31

The question may still remain in the minds of many: How, then, shall we teach or preach from the prophets of the Old Testament? Few passages have been of greater help and comfort to me personally than Isaiah 40. It is by all accounts my favorite chapter.

This chapter fits best under the genre of a salvation message in the great promise-plan of God. It begins in verses 1–2 with a modified form of the messenger formula: "Comfort, comfort my people, says your God. Speak tenderly to Jerusalem."

Then come the words of salvation in verse 2: "Proclaim to her that her service has been completed, that her sin has been paid for, that she has received from the Lord's hand double for all her sins."

But what is the basis for such a bold series of declarations? That rationale comes from an unidentified voice that calls out for all mortals to clear the path and to fill in the valleys in preparation for the arrival of the King of kings. These metaphors of road building point to the spiritual and moral preparation that is required if we are to get ready for the arrival of the Messiah, much as the ancients cleared the route that was to be taken by the arriving ruler of their day. So what will happen, and what is the basis for the words of salvation? Verse 5 answers that by affirming that "The glory of the Lord will be revealed, and all mankind together will see it. For the mouth of the Lord has spoken."

True, people are beautiful, and they do flourish like the flowers of the field, but only for a brief moment (vv. 6–8). Our hope and confidence is not in people, who often vacillate so widely.

Our security for this word of grace and promise is in "The word of our God [which] stands forever" (v. 8b).

With this prologue, the prophet launches into one of the most fantastic series of declarations and reassurances that one can find in all of Scripture on "Our Incomparably Great God." The title or subject of our message comes from the repeated question that forms a heading for each of the final two strophes in verses 18 and 25. They ask, "To whom, then, will you compare God?" and "'To whom will you compare me? Or who is my equal?' says the Holy One." These verses also serve as the focal point of the passage and therefore give us the subject for our sermon or teaching lesson.

Focal Point: Isaiah 40:18, 25

Homiletical Key Word: Comparisons

Interrogative: What? (*What* are the inadequate comparisons we make to our Lord who is incomparably great in all that he is and does?)

The teacher and exegete will find three clearly marked strophes in verses 12–31. They may be outlined as follows:

I. Introduction: Our Incomparably Great God
   A. In His Power over Us (vv. 12–17)
      1. Compared to All of Nature (v. 12)
      2. Compared to the Wisdom of Individuals (vv. 13–14)
      3. Compared to the Muscle of Nations (vv. 15–17)
   B. In His Personal Being toward Us (vv. 18–24)
      1. Compared to Inert Idols (vv. 18–20)
      2. Compared to Princes and Nobles (vv. 21–24)
   C. In His Pastoral Care/Provisions for Us (vv. 25–30)
      1. Compared to All Finite Things (vv. 25–26)
      2. Compared to Despondent Persons (vv. 27–28)
      3. Compared to the Strength of Youths (vv. 29–30)
II. Conclusion (v. 31)

❖

This oracle of salvation, after it is introduced in verses 1–8, begins with a shout for those who are bringing the good news of the gospel: Get up on a high mountain and announce as forth-rightly as possible, "Here is your God!" (v. 9). It is an epiphany, an appearance of the mightiest person in all the universe: Here comes the Lord and ruler of all.

What follows in verses 10 and 11 is much like what an over-ture is to a whole symphony. It states the themes that will be unfolded in the three strophes that follow (which we have just outlined above). First, it declares that the sovereign Lord comes with power and ruling authority that brooks no rivals (v. 10a). That theme will be taken up in the first strophe of verses 12–17. But then the overture continues in verse 10b, noting that God is not a philosophy, a force, or even a doctrine; he is a living person! His reward is with him and his recompense accompa-nies him, for he has been aware of all that has gone on while he has been away. This theme of God as the living God who exceeds all idols, princes, rulers, and nobles is set forth in the second strophe of verses 18–24. But for the moment the theme is merely introduced and hinted at until the prophet can get to its full announcement. Finally, the overture-like introduction concludes in verse 11 with a note about how pastoral and ten-der this coming one is, for he is one who can and will provide his flock with all that they need. That is the last theme that will be developed in the strophe of verses 25–31. We are now ready for the grand symphony of these themes themselves in verses 12–31.[6]

The overture to our message having been concluded, we begin with the first of our three attempted comparisons in verse 12. Our God is incomparable in his *power.*

The first candidate for attempting to match our God is nature. Five questions are raised in attempting to cover the entire range of possible challenges to the power of God. Thus, the bulk of the seven oceans is in comparison to our Lord just a handful of water in the hollow of his hand. The celestial heavens are in compar-ison also reduced to the space between his thumb and little fin-ger. All the dust and dirt of the earth is not more than a third of a bushel basket if we are really thinking in terms of the Triune God of the whole universe. No less outweighed are the moun-tains and the hills of the earth, for our Lord is so much greater than these piles of rock, snow, ice, and dirt that he can put them on his scales and easily balance them out. So why are we so intimidated by all the pretenders to power in our day? If our God so easily outclasses all of nature, which tends to cause our amazement, why do we not believe he can meet any and every challenge in life?

But it may not be nature that threatens and intimidates us; instead, it may be the intelligence and wisdom of people. Can our God keep up with all the computers and the research of the modern period? Five more questions are asked in verses 13–14. They ask whether God has ever consulted one of us in a supposed moment of his deficiency. Did he ever take a degree from one of our schools? The whole series of questions is so rhetorical and so silly that to ask them is to have an immediate answer: God alone is the source of all wisdom, so why would he be frightened or intimidated by all these lesser peons?

Three similes follow in verse 15 to show us that not even the nations in all their pomp and circumstance compare to the living God, for the nations' powers are like a "drop in a bucket," and they, in comparison to our God, are treated "as dust on the scales"; indeed, as "fine dust." So much for military powers, drug cartels, and economic wealth. They really are not worth our worry in comparison to the power we find in our living God.

Can we build a model that would match the power of our God? Verse 16 suggests we take the famous cedar trees of Lebanon (which would be like taking the redwood trees of California) and all the animals of that famous cattle raising area (like that of Texas) and construct a huge sacrifice to match our view of the greatness of God. Let it be seventy-five miles wide and long and twenty-five miles high. Then light a fire on it as an altar and say, "That's how big my idea of God is!" But it would not be sufficient to match either the power or the grandeur of our Lord. Before him, all nations, all nature, all wisdom, and even all models of our God are so minute, insignificant, and terribly inadequate they cannot express anywhere near the real magnificence of our God.

But what about God's personhood? Verses 18–24 take up the challenge to offer other comparisons to our God. Who can we put up as a contender for his *person*?

Certainly the idols cannot be serious contenders, though verses 19–20 explore this thought for the moment. An objection is heard from contemporary readers of Isaiah's message: "Skip this point, for we do not have icons in our backyards to whom we offer our Wheaties cereal every morning; idolatry is just not our cup of tea!" But wait a minute. Idolatry is a universal problem, for the essence of idolatry is coveting. Anytime we place any person, thing, or goal in a position that is equal to or greater than God, we are in the throes of idolatry.

Actually, Isaiah has a lot of fun with this charge. For those who are too poor to have a craftsman make an idol with gold overlay and silver necklaces, he advises that the wood selected for this cheaper variety be selected with great care. It would be embarrassing to have one's god destroyed by termites. Oh yes, get a craftsman who has some skill. Some workers couldn't make a god if their life depended on it. One thing more: Nail your god down to the floor, for one needs stability above all else in a deity. Isaiah is probably remembering the god Dagon, which came unglued in the presence of the ark of the covenant of God in the Philistine territory in the days of Samuel. So nail down your god! The irony ought to have been obvious to all. God is not dead wood; he is a living person!

But if the personhood of idols is a non sequitur, what can be said about kings and princes (vv. 21–24)? They too forget that the God of the universe sits enthroned above the circle of the earth. Nothing escapes his notice or his attention. Princes, kings, governors, judges, and all others in authority come, but they also leave office and this life just as quickly. Some hardly get started in office. Then they are gone. Why? Because God blows on them, and that is the end of them. They are removed both from office and from the earth.

So why are we frightened and intimidated by all these empty masks of our day? Is it because we think they are more real than God is? What a major mistake for Israel to make; what a major mistake for us to repeat!

The final comparison attempted concerns the *pastoral care* or *provision* that our God is able to give to us (vv. 25–31). Once more, the writer under the inspiration of God demands, "'To whom will you compare me? Or who is my equal?' says the Holy One."

For example, take the stars. Do any of us have any idea who created all of them (v. 26)? "God," we all answer in chorus. Correct! He brings them out each evening with such regularity that our watches are set by the pattern of the solar system. More than that, he calls each star by name. But that raises another question: Are there more stars in the heavens than there are people in the world? By a huge majority, there are millions and billions more stars than the six billion plus people in the world. So if God knows all those billions of stars by name, why do I think that he does not know me by name, I who am made in his image and redeemed by his grace? Since only parents can name their children, God is the parent and creator of the stars, for he named them.

Still we object further, as do the despondent persons mentioned in verse 27. They think that God has disregarded them and their rights. But they too have forgotten that the everlasting God does not grow weary or tired from all the work of running the universe. No one can put a regulator on his understanding, his compassion, or his tender care for people who are hurting. Our God is fantastically great and beyond any comparison of any magnitude. He is the source of all strength that all—from infants to those who are in the pride of health—need.

Why then do we put our hope and confidence in anything else? Those who put their total trust in the God who is above all gods, all lords, all powers, and all competitors are those who will soar, run, and walk instead of fainting and despairing.

Our God is infinitely great and beyond comparison to anything or anyone we have ever thought or imagined. It is to him we should bow and in reverence give thanksgiving and praise. We confess that all other competitors are cheap imitations that we should never elevate to a place anywhere near our Lord's. Our God is an awesome God!

Conclusion

The power of preaching and teaching from the prophets hardly can be appreciated if one has done little or no examination of these texts. The sheer bulk of the words of the prophets is almost equal to the whole New Testament. But besides the extensive space they occupy in the revelation of God, they carry an extraordinary amount of clout with regard to both the threat-ened judgment of God and his promised redemption and deliv-erances, both in the present and the future.

To cut the church off from these words would be to let the church float in the air, rootless and without a history or an anchor in space and time. The church must be connected with the promises made to Israel in the past. To preach these words faithfully is to unleash for God's people direction, comfort, and a hope that surpasses every other expectation that mortals could ever imagine or aspire to on planet earth!

8

Preaching and Teaching the Laments of the Old Testament

The two broad categories of genres in the Old Testament are prose and poetry. Poetry easily divides into wisdom and psalms, with psalms exhibiting both lament and praise as its two main divisions. Since we are mainly concerned with laments in this chapter, it is best we explore what is meant by lament, then note where laments are found in the Old Testament, study the form of the lament, and finally ask how one can teach or preach from a lament.

What Is a Lament?

Biblical laments have been categorized since the early days of form criticism (under Gunkel[1] and Begrich[2]) as individual laments and community laments. The reasons for distinguishing these two categories is to determine whether the lament is from a single individual or represents the issues that were present in the community.

This may seem quite straightforward; however the first-person pronoun speaker, "I," in the Psalms often acts as a representative for the whole group. Or, if the lament is from the king, he too could be a representative of the whole group.

Given the fact that the lament is a poetic genre, it shares many features of poetry. Traditionally, Hebrew poetry has been characterized by its distinctive emphasis on the balancing of ideas between the lines (called Hebrew parallelism) rather than on possessing a distinct rhythmic pattern. In fact, to this day, no one school of thought on rhythm or meter has been able to convince the other schools that it has discovered the proper formula for defining Hebrew poetic meter. None who profess to have found what the meter is will tell us the formula so that we all can observe it. Instead, they want to show us how they personally work it out in selected texts.

Some believe that the meter can be determined by watching the stressed and unstressed syllables (Holscher, Mowinckel, Horst, and Segert). Others argue that the key to locating meter is to be found in the accents and not in the stressed Hebrew syllables (Ley, Sievers). Still others focus on the number of syllables per line of Hebrew text (Freedman). It may well be, after all, that Hebrew poetry, like Ugaritic/Canaanite poetry, does not have any meter, as G. D. Young successfully argued years ago.

Hebrew poetry does have parallelism (a balance of ideas). We are disappointed, however, to learn that Hillers[3] found that 104 out of 266 lines in Lamentations (39 percent) exhibited no form of parallelism, unless one counted synthetic or formal parallelism. Synthetic or formal Hebrew parallelism occurs when the poetic lines are placed side by side to form one complete sentence with an artificial break in the sentence to form the two lines. The problem this creates is that it is often difficult, if not impossible, to decide syntactically where the line division (*caesura*) comes. This will affect meaning and commentary in those cases.

While this chapter generally is dubious with regard to the question of the presence of meter in Hebrew poetry, it can affirm that Karl Budde's 1882 identification and definition of *qinah* meter has tended to stand.[4] This hollow, or limping, kind of verse tends to be associated with poems of lament. In the *qinah* pattern, the first poetic line is at least one word or grammatical unit longer than the second line, thereby giving us the most typical pattern of 3 + 2, but also patterns of 4 + 3 or even 4 + 2. For example, in Lamentations 3:4–5 there is a typical 3 + 2 pattern (hyphenated words represent one Hebrew word).

	1	2	3
v. 4	"He-wore-out he-broke	my-flesh my-bones	and-my-skin . . . .
v. 5	He-has-besieged with-bitterness	and-encircled and-hardship	around-me . . . ."

The effect that the missing third element in the second line creates is one of hollowness or a limping gait. It is like waiting for the other shoe to fall, but it never does. This format adds to the dark mood and heavyheartedness that matches the content of the poem.

Where Are Laments Found in the Old Testament?

The Book of Lamentations is arguably the principal example of the lament form. Lamentations is a communal lament (except for chap. 3) and is therefore similar to other community laments found in the Old Testament. Some good examples of such *communal* laments are: Psalms 44; 60; 74; 79; 80; 83; and 89; Isaiah 63; Jeremiah 14; and Habakkuk 1. Other psalms with a partial community lament are Psalms 68; 82; 85; 90; 106; and 115.

Far more extensive are the examples of *individual* laments. Some representatives of this genre would be: Psalms 3–7; 10–14; 16–17; 22–23; 25–28; 31; 35–36; 38–43; 51–59; 61–64; 69; 71; 73; 77; 86; 88; 102; 109; 120; and 130; Jeremiah 11; 15; 17–18; 20; numerous texts in Job; and, of course, Lamentations 3.

The Form of the Lament

Most agree that there is some flexibility in the order in which the various lament elements appear and the number of times a single element may appear. However, here are the seven classic elements in a lament that tend to appear with some regularity.

1. An invocation
2. A plea to God for help
3. One or more complaints

4. Confession of sin or an assertion of one's innocency
5. An imprecation on one's enemies
6. Confidence that God will respond
7. A hymn or blessing

The focal point of the lament is in the one or more complaint elements, for this will often tell us why the writer even bothered to compose the lament. Just as Solomon's prayer set forth seven situations that could call forth prayer in the temple (1 Kings 8), so it would appear that four of his seven situations would also serve as bases for offering a lament to God in the event of national disasters.[5] These four were: (1) defeat in battle (vv. 33–34), (2) drought (vv. 35–36), (3) other natural disasters or disease (vv. 37–40), and (4) captivity (vv. 46–50). An example of such a complaint can be seen in Psalm 73:13.

> Surely in vain have I kept my heart pure;
>   in vain have I washed my hands in innocence.

Another can be seen in Psalm 120:2.

> Save me, O LORD, from lying lips
>   and from deceitful tongues.

Often the invocation to a lament is combined with the plea to God for help, as in Psalm 7:1.

> O LORD my God, I take refuge in you;
>   save and deliver me from all who pursue me.

Psalm 13:1 provides another example.

> How long, O LORD? Will you forget me forever?
>   How long will you hide your face from me?

The confession of sin or the assertion of innocence can be illustrated in Psalm 7:3–5.

> O LORD my God, if I have done this
>   and there is guilt on my hands—

> If I have done evil to him who is at peace with me,
>   or without cause have robbed my foe—
> then let my enemy pursue and overtake me;
>   let him trample my life to the ground
> and make me sleep in the dust. Selah.

An imprecation or curse on one's enemies can be seen in Psalm 109:8–10.

> May his days be few;
>   may another take his place of leadership.
> May his children be fatherless
>   and his wife a widow.
> May his children be wandering beggars;
>   may they be driven from their ruined homes.

Finally, a hymn or blessing is seen in Psalm 109:30–31.

> With my mouth I will greatly extol the LORD;
>   in the great throng I will praise him.
> For he stands at the right hand of the needy one,
>   to save his life from those who condemn him.

Laments run the gamut of emotions, from complaints, to protestations of innocence, to praise to God for his deliverance. God, who hears the complaint, is the same God who responds with assurances of pardon and help, thereby eliciting a hymn of praise to the God of blessing.

Why Study or Preach from Laments?

God has placed personal and national laments in Scripture, it would appear, as a corrective against euphoric, celebratory notions of faith, which romantically portray life as consisting only of sweetness and light. Such a one-sided, happiness-only view fails to deal with the realities of life. It drives the hurtful and painful side of life into the corners of faith and practice, leaving few guides or comforts from mortals or the Word of God.

On the contrary, God has given us in the laments of Scripture a solace where the full spectrum of our earthly journey can be represented. This is especially true of the Book of Lamentations. Lamentations is a deeply emotional book. It openly acknowledges the presence of weeping (1:2), desolation (1:4), mockery (1:7), groaning (1:8), hunger (1:11), and grief (2:11), just to name a few of the pains and sorrows encountered there. Some feel the book lacks spontaneity, since it is one of the most formal books of the Old Testament. Its first four chapters are arranged into twenty-two stanzas, each in the form of an alphabetic acrostic, with only chapter 5 not participating in the acrostic, despite the fact that the fifth chapter also has twenty-two verses. One can imagine how much work it took to construct four alphabetic acrostics for Lamentations.

But a deep, genuine expression of emotion does not require spontaneity.[6] Unpondered prayers, which have not been written out or premeditated, are not always the most real, passionate, heartfelt, genuine, or alive prayers. Instead, our emotions are like a river that flows out of our heart, and the forms used are like the banks of the river that allow it to gain some depth. Without those "banks," those forms that give structure to our emotions, our feelings would become shallow and flood all over the place. But the structure of the alphabetic acrostic, rather than inhibiting earnestness and real depth, provides the categories in which the river can run deep.

All too frequently we fault form and order in worship services when the real culprit is the dry spring of our own hearts. Therefore, in times of grief and trouble, it may be well to let the river run deep in our praying, preaching, and conversation.

In this way, Lamentations, like the other laments, forces us to deal with suffering by directing our despair not *away* from God, but *toward* him. It also performs the pastoral work of comforting us without downplaying the human realities of suffering and pain. Sometimes, it is also necessary to deal with guilt that accompanies pain. But Lamentations always acknowledges the real presence of the hurt and urges us to "talk it out" in the presence of God. God's presence is promised right where the pain, grief, and hurt are. In the end we learn that it is the Lord alone who is our portion (Lam. 3:24).

Some are troubled by the use of the acrostic form. Is this to aid Israel's memory of the nightmare of destruction in 586 B.C.? Hardly! Any Jew who was there, and all who followed, could never forget the loss and pain suffered (anymore than this nation will ever forget September 11, 2001) as the nation, the temple, the throne, and the house of David, so it appeared for the moment, all went into oblivion.

The acrostic is there to help God's people work through every facet of grief and suffering, from A to Z as we would say using our English alphabet. It must all be itemized and exposed completely. But it must also be remembered that grief and pain are not sovereign or endless; there is a terminus. Without this *finis*, God's people would be crippled and permanently frustrated. So the lament was given to help us cope with grief. In doing so, the Old Testament gives us the most comprehensive address to the problem of suffering from the standpoint of divine revelation to be found anywhere. Thus, Lamentations rejects stoicism and emotionless life. It, like Romans 12:15, urges us to "Rejoice with those who rejoice, [but] weep with those who weep" (NASB). Properly controlled emotions are not obnoxious to God; at times we must weep!

How to Teach or Preach from a Lament

Lamentations 2

This chapter provides a good example of a lament, not because it illustrates every characteristic of a lament, for it does not, but rather because it shows how flexible this form, like most genres, really is.

Sermon/Teaching Title: "Taking Suffering Personally"

Text: Lamentations 2:1–22

Focal Point: Verse 17: "The LORD has done what he had planned; he has fulfilled his word, which he decreed long ago. He has overthrown you without pity, he has let the enemy gloat over you, he has exalted the horn of your foes."

Homiletical Key Word: Reasons

Interrogative: Why?

I. (No Invocation)
II. Complaints
  A. Because Suffering Comes from the Lord (vv. 1–10)
  B. Because Suffering Affects God's Servant (vv. 11–13)
III. Confession of Sin
  A. Because Suffering Provokes Such Personal Responses (vv. 14–19)
  B. Because Suffering Makes Its Complaint to the Lord (vv. 20–22)
IV. (No Curse on the Enemy)
V. (No Hymn or Blessing)

Too many do-gooders with misguided kindness advise: "Don't take suffering personally. Don't think anything about it." The truth is that suffering is intensely personal. The first ten verses of Lamentations 2 have forty references to God's judgment or anger at the sin that forced this rebuke. However, God's anger is measured and controlled by his love and justice. It is God's expression of his outrage at sin while it is also his expression of his continued caring for us.

Psalm 120

A second example of a lament can be seen in Psalm 120, the first of the fifteen psalms of ascent. Here are the elements of lament in this psalm.

1. An Invocation: "I call on the Lord in my distress, / and he answers me" (v. 1).
2. A Plea to God for Help: "Save me, O Lord, from lying lips / and from deceitful tongues" (v. 2).
3. A Curse of Enemies (Imprecation): "What will he do to you, / and what more besides, O deceitful tongue?" (v. 3).
4. Confidence in God's Response: "He will punish you with a warrior's sharp arrows, / with burning coals of the broom tree" (v. 4).
5. Assertion of Innocence: "Woe to me that I dwell in Meshech, / that I live among the tents of Kedar! / Too long have I lived / among those who hate peace. / I am a man of peace; / but when I speak, they are for war" (vv. 5–7).

Sermon/Teaching Title: "Finding a Way to Handle Slander"
Text: Psalm 120:1–7
Focal Point: Verse 2: "Save me, O LORD, from lying lips and from deceitful tongues."
Homiletical Key Word: Ways
Interrogative: How?

I. Our Cry for Help Must Be to the Lord (vv. 1–2)
II. Our Confidence Must Be That God Will Respond (vv. 3–4)
III. Our Quest for Peace Must Be Constant (vv. 5–7)

Slander is as lethal a weapon as a revolver! Therefore, as the Israelite pilgrims journeyed to the religious festivals in Jerusalem, they could not help wondering whether they would be victims of a vicious smear campaign at home while they were gone.

But why was this subject put first in this collection of pilgrim psalms? Samuel Cox answered, "It is hardly an exaggeration to say that half of the miseries of human life spring from the reckless and malignant use of the tongue. And these wicked tongues generally wag fastest behind a [person's] back. . . . We judge these sins of the tongue all too lightly, until we ourselves are injured by them."[7]

Psalm 77

This sermon from Psalm 77 by the Rev. Dr. Dorington Little was preached on January 21, 2001, at the First Congregational Church, Hamilton, Massachusetts.[8] It provides an excellent example of how to preach from a lament.

During the War of 1812, Captain Charles Barnard sailed from New York to the southern seas to engage in sealing. Upon arrival, he and his crew discovered and rescued a group of shipwrecked British sailors on an island near the Falklands.

Although their two countries were at war, arrangements were worked out to return the British seamen to their homeland. But in order to do so, additional provisions were needed. So Captain Barnard and a small crew of the rescued sailors landed on another nearby island to spend a few days looking for supplies to feed his now full ship.

To his dismay, as he tromped about, his newly rescued guests deliberately sailed off, leaving him all alone. It seems that they liked his ship and crew better than they liked him. They even took his extra clothes, his coat, his blanket, his sealskins, his tools, his weapons, his powder horn for making fire, and even his hunting dog. All this was done in a calculated effort to make sure he died in the wasteland.

Standing on a high hill, he watched as his now-captured boat sailed out of sight and he yelled out at the top of his lungs his parting shot, *"Go, then, for you are all bad fellows!"* Later, he referred to them as *"cold-hearted British"* with *"deaf ears"* and *"impenetrable hearts,"* perpetrating an *"unparalleled act of baseness."*

Well, there he remained, all alone on an uninhabited island—for what would amount to two years—surviving like Robinson Crusoe. Fully aware of the stark and bleak realities before him, on the first night of his desertion, Barnard says he laid down and *"prayed to God to direct and inspire me with fortitude to submit with patience to this **doubly afflictive trial.**"* [9]

"Doubly afflictive trials"—an expression of quaint redundancy, don't you think? Even still, we know exactly what it means since we all have them. All of us, in our view, have doubly afflictive trials, which in turn, elicit a certain emotional and spiritual response.

Today we're going to look at a response to certain trials as recorded by the psalmist named Asaph. Asaph, you may know, wrote twelve of the psalms. [10] A member of the tribe of Levi, King David placed him in charge of the worship music in the tent of meeting . . . prior to the building of the temple.

A composer with striking and courageous candor, he describes his faith, which falters and struggles as it faces the perplexities of life; the doubly afflictive trials! As such, Psalm 77—read in its entirety earlier in the service—is an honest response to feelings of being abandoned by God. In fact, it is a psalm with which all of us can probably identify at some point. The reason for this is that it exudes a practical realism. It laments. It cries. It hurts. It anguishes. In it, faith does not always consist only of positive affirmations and feelings. Rather, here we see faith hammered in the tough arena of real life. Experiences of anguish and even befuddlement are not foreign to the psalmist. Here the psalmist cries out, and yet in that very process he is brought to see how God has been at work and will yet be at work. For you see, the psalm is more than emotion. It is emotion checked by the motions or actions of God on behalf of his people.

Now, the exact historical circumstances of this particular psalm of Asaph are unknown to us. Is this the result of a horrible trauma on a national scale, or is this a cry of pain in a strictly personal context? We don't really know. Still, whatever the background, the psalm poignantly speaks. What do we hear it say to us?

God's People Can and Do Cry Out with Anguish and Doubt (vv. 1–9)

First, in verses 1–9 we discover that there are times when God's people can and do cry out with anguish and doubt. Literally, the psalm opens, "My voice, to the Lord, I am crying out, my voice to the Lord." This is Asaph's prayer. The piling up of words and expressions is all calculated to present us with unmitigated anguish. This is a haunting, mournful cry. It won't go away. It is not a passing sorrow. There is a lingering span of pain to this ordeal. It persistently begs for attention and care.

So the psalmist prays. He seeks the Lord, with hands outstretched to the heavens. With unwearying voice and untiring hands, he calls out and reaches up to God, again and again and again, for his soul, he says, "refused to be comforted."

But the problem, as verse 3 shows us, is that when he thinks of God, he is not particularly comforted: "I remembered you, O God, and I groaned; I mused, and my spirit grew faint. *Selah.*" ("Selah" indicates a musical pause—remember, this is worship!) God's inattentiveness to Asaph's immediate needs leaves him faint. He finds no consolation.

Now, it seems strange to us, perhaps even embarrassing, that God does not respond. After all, do we not say that God answers prayer? And isn't it odd to us that the very remembering of God does not bring peace to the heart—but turmoil instead?

Yet that is the case here. And so it is sometimes with us—if we're brutally honest. Sometimes, we too are in that crying state. We come again and again to our God, and there is no answer. Therefore, the thought of God troubles us rather than consoles us. It hurts rather than heals.

Perhaps in this we are even sleepless! And just like the psalmist in verse 4, we think that God has kept us from sleep, that He holds and props open our eyelids to prolong our suffering. God doesn't even grant the escape from inner suffering that deep sleep often provides. Instead, we lie in bed and mentally muse over better songs from better times (vv. 5–6)—but that too does us no good. Our voice may be silenced, but the heart unceasingly broods, even rhythmically pounds out its complaint. Thump-thump. Thump-thump. Thump-thump.

So ultimately, the big question is raised in our spirits. It cannot be avoided. It spews forth, surrounded by six rhetorical handmaidens in verses 7–9:

1. Will the Lord reject forever?
2. Will he never show his favor again?
3. Has his unfailing love vanished forever?
4. Has his promise failed for all time?
5. Has God forgotten to be merciful?
6. Has he in anger withheld his compassion?

There it is! It is all out in the open now. All the misgivings come to the surface. They bubble over and cannot be contained. While, surely, the answer to these is no, there is, nevertheless, a hint of something else lurking beneath the surface, a larger question, simmering in the dark waters of the soul.

Do you see the real issue here? It is doubt. The psalmist is saying, "Here is my pain. There is my God. This is my voice. So where is his answer? Will he answer?"

Has he rejected me?
Has he forgotten me?
What about his love?

What about his promises?
What about his mercy?
Is it all anger now?
Is that all I can really expect from him?
Dark doubt—does God really care?

Be sure, this is not doubt that God exists. Asaph does not doubt that. That is more modern than ancient. That is post-Enlightenment and sub-biblical. But Asaph does doubt that God cares for him or for his nation.

Again, this is not an unusual struggle for the Christian. There are times when we wonder where God is and what God is doing. How can he do this to us? How can he leave us, seemingly, in the lurch? Why is he so apparently inconsistent and inconstant?

Yes, we admit that there are times of doubt, and from the psalmist we learn that it is better to talk about them than to stifle them. Of course we must be careful here. While Asaph gives us permission to express our emotion to God, he does not give us permission to sin in the process. And there are times when he himself repents of his emotions (cf. Ps. 73:21–22).

In this case, Alexander MacLaren's wise counsel applies: "Doubts are better put into plain speech than lying diffused and darkening, like poisonous mists, in the heart . . . expressing them is like cutting a channel in a bog for the water to run."[11]

And that's what verses 1–9 are like—like water running out of the bog of Asaph's perplexed, suffering mind and spirit. These are words giving vent to his emotions and his pain, words expressing his doubts.

Now, if we were left here—at the end of verse 9—then we would be left in a very difficult place. We would be left in futility and not faith. But we are not! Look at verses 10–15.

GOD'S PEOPLE MOVE ON TO CLARIFY THEIR PERSPECTIVE (VV. 10–15)

In verses 10–15 we see that while God's people vent their anguish from time to time, they also move on to clarify their perspective. Verse 10 is the turning point in the psalm. It is a bit

cryptic, but it may be read something like, "It is my grief that
the right hand of the Most High has changed." If so, then it goes
with the preceding complaints—he thinks that God has changed.
There is no sure footing on which to stand on, for God is fickle.

Or, it can read as it does here in the NIV—as an appeal to the
stability of God. If so, then it functions like a hinge between the
two major sections of the psalm. It swings us from despairing
introspection (and possible futility) to uplifting meditation (and
the eventual reaffirmation of faith).

The psalmist says that he is thinking (v. 10) and remembering (v. 11) and meditating (v. 12) and considering (v. 12) God—
not himself, not his condition, not his pain, not his turmoil. No,
now he is making the supreme effort to contemplate God.

Underscoring this effort is the fact that in verses 11–12 the
verbs are repeated: remember/remember and meditate/consider.
This intensifies the intention of the psalmist. In his battle with
doubt and despair, he knows that relief is only found by a deliberate fighting to remember God first and foremost. This is
Asaph's strategy, both for himself and for his people.[12]

I learned the other day that in the Hebrew Bible there really
is no word for *doubt*. On the other hand, there are many words
to express wonder and awe and amazement—at who God is and
what he has done. "Thus the mind-surpassing grandeur of the
reality of God prevented the power of doubt from setting up its
own independent dynasty."[13]

I think this is why, in this psalm, all of a sudden there is a dramatic shift from morbid introspection to divine meditation. If
you take a moment to count, the first-person singular pronouns
"I," "my," or "me" dominate the first six verses, occurring some
eighteen times in the NIV. But from verse 13 onward, God dominates. He is mentioned no less than twenty-one times! He is
now the theme, not personal affliction. Now the view is of God's
deeds, God's miracles, God's works—and above all—God's holy
ways (v. 12).

And to ponder all this is to realize that God is incomparable
(v. 13). He is incomparable because he is a redeeming God who
pours out his power on behalf of his people. His mighty arm
really is at work on their behalf (v. 15). All this must be remembered if we are to have any hope and ability to cope with our
own circumstances. Without this we are confined to despair and

futility and the freight of our mortality. But this is the biblical process by which we escape the despair of the soul. We remember God. We review the works of God. We worship God.

His ways are holy, meaning they are perfect and just all the time even though we do not perfectly comprehend them. He is always above reproach. And we take comfort in recalling the fact that we are his people (v. 15). As such, we irrevocably belong to him. That is the clarifying perspective we need.

GOD'S PEOPLE REMEMBER THEIR REDEMPTION (vv. 16–19)

Now, look at verses 16–19. There we see the details of precisely what God has done to redeem his people. Yes, God's people may vent their anguish from time to time, but God's people must move on to clarify their perspective, and that is done chiefly by remembering their redemption.

You know what this is! The redemption depicted here is the great action of God on behalf of his people at the crossing of the Red Sea. This was their defining moment (Exod. 14). This is when God called them out from Egypt and spectacularly delivered them. At the very moment when they feared being annihilated, when they were cringing on the shore of the sea, caught between it and a ferocious, advancing army—at the very moment of their deepest terror—God showed up, so to speak.

Moses raised his staff over the sea, and the waters parted. Walled in on each side by formidable sea, the Hebrews passed through to the other side. And the Egyptians who followed were swallowed up by the waves, as God delivered his people from their enemies.

Yes, as the psalmist says, the waters writhed and convulsed. The clouds poured rain, the heavens thundered, God's lightning shot out like arrows, and the earth shook and quaked. All this was done to form a path through the sea to redeem a puny people.

That's what God did—he who is a holy, great, caring, mighty God. That's who he is, and so that's what he did. And that's the redemption that the psalmist recalls as a result of his clarifying perspective! This is what gives him hope that his present and his future are in God's hands—God's sea-parting, redeeming, saving, caring hands.

In his hour of dark doubt, in his pain, here is his God. This is his voice. This is his answer. This is his answer to the doubts expressed back in verses 7–9:

Has he forgotten?	*No.*
What about his love?	*It is real.*
What about his promises?	*They are true.*
What about his mercy?	*Depend on it.*
Is he all anger?	*Don't be silly.*
Does God really care?	*Absolutely!*

Look no further than to his redeeming acts!

And so it is for us. On days of dark doubt, when we need a clarifying perspective, we look to God, and we remember. We remember the supreme act of redemption to which the Red Sea pointed. "My voice" in verse 1 is drowned out by the "thunder" of God's redeeming voice (v. 18). We remember his sinless Son's aching, bleeding arms outstretched on a splintered cross for our sin. We recall the beauty of undeserved grace. We allow ourselves to be caught up in the wonder of it all, despite it all. God has spoken. Really. And "in these last days he has spoken to us by his Son" (Heb. 1:2).

Does this wipe out our circumstances?

Does this obliterate our pain?

Of course not—but it reminds us that God does care, he is not powerless, and he will yet again sustain and deliver his people. Our trouble is not forgotten; it is merely dwarfed by a greater reality.[14] Pain is not the sum total of the journey. In the midst of pain, all may seem muddled, but our God has spoken and will yet deliver us. So much so that as we meditate and muse and remember, we too can say, "Your ways, O God, are holy. What god is so great as our God?" (Ps. 77:13), and "If God is for us, who can be against us?" (Rom. 8:31).

GOD'S PEOPLE EXPRESS THEIR ULTIMATE CONFIDENCE (v. 20)

Now, as we conclude, look at the last verse of the psalm. As a result of remembering the deeds of our God, we see that God's people express their ultimate confidence.

"You led your people like a flock by the hand of Moses and Aaron" (v. 20).

That's what God did.

And that's what God does.

So that's our ultimate confidence. We move from doubt and despair to God, his redeeming power, and thus on to confidence—in God. God leads his people. He is our good shepherd, even Jesus. And we are his flock, his sheep, who need his constant care and wisdom. And so we are reminded of the fact that his redeeming guidance and care are our confidence for the present and the future.

Given that, verse 20 is not really, in my view, an anticlimactic postscript. Instead, this is the point to which the entire psalm leads us and points us and drives us. Instead of being torn to pieces on the rocks of doubt, we are led by the Lord, even carried as sheep in our gentle shepherd's arms.

You see, while verses 1–2 are a picture of the restlessness of the despairing soul—one that cannot see beyond itself—verse 20 is the picture of the soul that recalls God and thus returns to trust God. It is trust reinforced and prompted by biblical, God-centered meditation.

This soul is led by God.

This is where we stand.

This is our sure foundation: God's shepherding care.

Therefore, upon this we meditate.

Brothers and sisters, as a practical postscript, this is why biblical meditation is so important. It acquaints us with God's ways so that we will trust him when life is tough. And as we've noted on another occasion, Scripture memorization and biblical meditation are different—although intertwined and inseparable. A simple analogy helps to clarify what I mean.

In your kitchen you have cupboards. Why? Because in those cupboards you stock up on all the healthy foods that your family likes to eat—Fruit Loops, Cocoa Puffs, Cheese Puffs, and five-pound bars of Toblerone. But in order to be nourished by these excellent(!) foods, you have to do more than merely put them in the cupboard; you have to take them out and eat them! They do you a minimal amount of good simply sitting on the shelves. Their value is best realized as they are consumed.

So it is with biblical meditation! Your memory is the chest or cupboard or cabinet in which you store the truths of God's Word. But meditation utilizes the cupboard. Meditation is the deliberate reaching in to feed and nourish your soul on dark, spiritually lean days—on truth that has been stockpiled. And that's what Asaph does here. That's what we must do.

Again, this soul is led by God.

This is where we stand.

This is our sure foundation: God's shepherding care.

Therefore, upon this we meditate.

Conclusion

The "reason" for the lament is generally found in the *ki* clause in Hebrew, for this particle is usually translated "for," or "because." While this will mark the complaint section, it will also give us the focal point of the lament and thus the subject for the entire sermon or teaching session.

The other elements of the passage will suggest the development of the subject suggested in the complaint or the focal point for the passage. As each main point in your outline emerges from each of these elements, make sure that the theological teaching in the lament about God and our relationship to him is not lost. Much of this teaching may be wrapped up in the imagery used by the lament, but that should not prevent you from showing what it is that God wishes to say to us through this genre and this particular text.

All too frequently we have only praise choruses as the central part of our worship services. But what shall we do for the person who comes to our services with a heavy heart? Will they never hear a word of solace and comfort from the gospel?

Let us include lament as another aspect of our preaching and teaching the whole counsel of God.

9

Preaching and Teaching Old Testament Torah

A significant portion of the church tends to assume that "the torah is obsolete for Christians today."[1] The thought is that Christianity is an innovative religion that has broken away from its Jewish antecedents, and especially from the Pentateuch, which is generally thought to be synonymous with the concept of "law"—in the sense of regulations and restrictions only. But all of this is too presumptuous, for the apostles argued that the Christian church was in direct continuity with the plan and purpose of God in the Old Testament. Moreover, biblical torah cannot be narrowly restricted to the concept of law in the European sense of French *loi*, German *Gesetz*, or even Greek *nomos*, for torah includes the promises of God made to the patriarchs and to all who followed after them, along with the guidance it gave for living all of life.

The Meaning of Torah

The problem with many Christians' concept of law is that it implies merely formal regulations, often with ritual associations, to which the Old Testament community was subjected if they wished to attain favor with God. It is this incorrect conclusion that has led many to pit legal instructions for life in the Torah over against the life of grace described in the New Testament. Such a dichotomy is clearly against the teaching of Scripture. Torah is much more than law. The word *torah* probably comes from a Hebrew verb, meaning "to point [out a direction that one should go in]." That is why in the Book of Proverbs, which has so much teaching based on the Torah, the instruction is connected so often with a "path." God's law was meant to be a light on one's path; it was to point a person in the direction he or she should go.

But there is more. To recognize the presence of directions for living in the Torah is not equal to describing the main thrust or purpose of the Pentateuch. It has a more important purpose, namely, tracing the progress of God's word of promise to his people. The laws, or better still, the directions, must be fully integrated within the total text and story of God's promise-plan.

Meanwhile, the wisdom and prophetic books of the Bible rely on the Torah as being foundational for all they teach and affirm. For these sections of the Bible, the heart of the divinely directed life has been laid out in the Mosaic revelation. This is evidenced by the many direct quotations and indirect allusions to the Pentateuch that can be found in the books of the prophets and the wisdom books.

The Relation of Promise to Torah

The doctrine of the promise-plan of God is increasingly seen as the overarching theme and keystone of the first five books of the Bible, if not of the whole Bible. The promise-plan can be defined as a declaration or word from God. It is God's word about what he would be and what he would do for the line of people he had called to be his agents for blessing the world and, therefore, what God would be and what he would do through that line of people for all the nations of the earth.

Three key moments set the tone for the rest of the unveiling of this plan in the Pentateuch: Genesis 3:15; 9:27; and 12:1–3. In these texts, God announced four gifts: (1) the promise of a posterity or a "seed," (2) the promise that God himself would come and "dwell" among the tents of Shem,[2] (3) the promise of the land of Canaan to those who were called to be agents who would transmit the promise, and (4) the promise of the good news, or the gospel itself, that in that seed all the nations of the earth would be blessed.

This theme of the promise did not come to an end when the narrative of the pre-patriarchal revelation in Genesis 1–11 or even the patriarchal stories of Genesis 12–50 came to an end. On the contrary, in the two focal points of the rest of the Pentateuch, namely, the exodus and the revelation of the law on Mount Sinai, it becomes clear what the blessing of the promise would involve. The newly formed nation of Israel would be referred to repeatedly as "my people." The reason for this close relationship with God would be located in the covenant God made with the patriarchs (Exod. 2:24; 3:6).

How, then, did promise relate to torah? It was always a relationship that emphasized the priority of promise over law. Therefore, just as the patriarchal promises preceded the giving of the law on Sinai, so belief, faith, and redemption had to be the context for any obedience to the directions that God gave at Sinai. That is how God's selection of Isaac was made: solely on the basis of God's purpose and not on the basis of the accumulated pious deeds of his father Abraham or of Isaac himself. Accordingly, God also chose between Isaac's twins even before they were born (Gen. 25:23) and had the opportunity to do right or wrong (Rom. 9:11–12).

The Narrative Framework of the Torah

The best way to allow the Torah to speak to our day is to recognize that the Pentateuch is essentially, or overwhelmingly, in a narrative form. This narrative is part of an ongoing story that embraces the whole of humanity as told from the divine perspective. As such, the narrative has a beginning, a middle, and a temporary end (with the final end held over indefinitely until we come to the climax of the kingdom of God).

This narrative begins with the so-called primeval history of Genesis 1–11. Under the theme of the blessing (Hebrew: brk) of God, the story begins with the blessing God gave to the created order

(Gen. 1:22) and the first human couple (v. 28). That blessing continued in Genesis 5:2 and was picked up again after the flood story in Genesis 9:1. Even without the use of the word "to bless" or "blessing," God's blessing was present in pledges such as Genesis 3:15 and 9:27.[3] When the promise was given to Abraham in Genesis 12:1–3, the word "bless" or "blessing" occurred five times! The connection between the pre-patriarchal "blessing" and the patriarchal "word" of promise could not have been more obvious.

Just as Yahweh was the God "who brought you out of Ur of the Chaldeans" (e.g., Gen. 15:7), so in giving the stipulations of the Decalogue, Yahweh announced, "I am [Yahweh] your God, who brought you out of Egypt" (Exod. 20:2). Thus, the law is given in the context of God's gracious activity. He manifests his grace before he makes his stipulations!

But what has troubled most readers and theologians of the Torah is not the continuity of the narrative but the diverse nature of the two covenants. The Abrahamic promise was filled with the gifts of free grace and blessings, but Sinai seemed to impose demands, obligations, and commands.

So strongly was this disjuncture felt that Gerhard von Rad[4] pointed to Deuteronomy 26:5–9 as the key credo of Israel, along with other credos (I-believe statements) such as Joshua 24:16–18, and contended that these credos supported this division between the covenants. Von Rad's point was that the events of Sinai, which he regarded as the heart of the Pentateuch, were explicitly left out of these credos, thus proving that the Sinai legislation belonged to an older and separate generation, appearing only in the later exilic period as the alleged "P" document. On this he was mistaken.

Von Rad's view was sharply challenged,[5] as it had to be, for the part von Rad said was missing could be found if one included the entirety of Deuteronomy 26, not just verses 5–9, and all of Joshua 24, not just verses 16–18. The fact is that the exodus was clearly connected with Sinai in Exodus 19:3–8 and 20:2–17.

Even after all these connections are admitted, the problem still seems to remain: How are the demands and stipulations in Exodus 20 to Numbers 10 to be integrated, if at all, with the blessings and promises of the pre-patriarchal and patriarchal materials in Genesis? Our best answer is to respond by noting how the same combination of promise and commands already existed as the fabric that held together the patriarchal narratives. For example, the following commands were easily encompassed in the patriarchal story of promise without any feeling of maladjustment:

Genesis 12:1   "Leave your country"
        15:9   "Bring me a heifer"
        17:1   "Walk before me and be blameless"
        22:2   "Take your son, your only son, . . . and go . . ."
        26:2   "Do not go down to Egypt; live in the land where I tell you to live"
        31:3   "Go back to the land of your fathers"
        35:11 "Be fruitful and increase" (Found earlier in Gen. 1:28 and 9:1—either a
               blessing or a command!)

Thus, as each command was preceded and made in the context of promise for the patriarchs, so the call for obedience in the Mosaic law was never the condition for inaugurating the covenant or for its maintenance. The Ten Commandments were given in the context of grace, for the God who issued the commands was the God who had just redeemed Israel from the land of Egypt. Thus, the law was no less a gift from God and was rightly celebrated as a gift in Psalm 1:2; 19:7–11; and all of 119. To the psalmists, the law was sweeter than honey and more desirable than much fine gold! Promise did not oppose God's law, for both promise and law came from the same covenant-making God. Neither did law provide a separate means, not even a hypothetical means, for obtaining salvation. Instead, the law provided a means for maintaining fellowship with God.

The Torah and Faith

Schmitt[6] has shown how the entire Pentateuch was unified with faith/belief as its linking device. At each of the perceived "compositional seams" of the Pentateuch, as Schmitt viewed them, the "faith-theme" (*Glaubens-Thematik*) appeared. Those compositional seams are as follows:

Genesis 15:6   "Abram believed the LORD, and he credited it to him as righteousness."
Exodus 4:5   "'This,' said the LORD, 'is so that you may believe that the LORD . . . has
               appeared to you.'"

Exodus 14:31	"The people feared the LORD and put their trust in him and in Moses his servant."
Numbers 14:11	"How long will they refuse to believe in me, in spite of all the miraculous signs?"
Numbers 20:12	"But the LORD said to Moses and Aaron, 'Because you did not trust in me enough to honor me as holy in the sight of the Israelites, you will not bring this community into the land I give them.'"
Deuteronomy 1:32	"In spite of this, you did not trust in the LORD your God."
Deuteronomy 9:23	"But you rebelled against the command of the LORD your God. You did not trust him or obey him."

Instead of viewing the Pentateuch as emphasizing the keeping of priestly law codes, Schmitt's study has taken a long stride toward demonstrating that the Pentateuch really intended to teach faith and belief in God and his promise. Obedience to the law, then, was the natural evidence that one had really trusted the Lord and believed his promise.

How to Preach and Teach Old Testament Torah

Given the large amount of narrative passages in the Torah, the strategy for interpreting those texts will be the same as we have already discussed in the chapter on preaching from narratives. But what about the legal texts? Do those texts disclose a distinction between law that is universal and timeless versus that which is temporal and culture-bound?

Most despair of finding any clear-cut division between those laws that are normative for all times and places and those that had a built-in obsolescence to them. But our interpretive problems will not absolve us in the final day, when we see our Lord, from pressing on to locate what most despair of finding: the normative principle in those texts that can be applied to all times and all cultures.

To begin with, the laws in Exodus 25 through Leviticus 16 are largely ceremonial. These laws seem to have little permanent relevance, other than the fact that they illustrate abiding truths. However, many do have parallel applications today (e.g., building a safety parapet around one's flat roof [Deut. 22:8] can today be applied to putting up a fence around your backyard swimming pool).

There was a clue to their temporary nature in the fact that these laws would be obsolete once the real truths to which they pointed replaced them. Thus, Exodus 25:9 and 25:40 clearly marked the tabernacle with its services and personnel as temporary, for they were only "models" or "patterns" that imitated what Moses was shown while he was on the mountain. The reality, Moses was taught, existed in heaven; he had made only a copy or a pattern of the heavenly reality. However, when the Messiah appeared, these copies had to be retired in favor of the new order of reality introduced by the person and work of Jesus. The Book of Hebrews makes just that point when it refers to the tabernacle and its ritual as "shadows" of the reality that was to come. But mind you, the Old Testament anticipated this and clearly put up the caution flag in Exodus 25:9 and 25:40 when this legislation was first given. There it claimed that the tabernacle with its services and sacrifices were merely copies or models of the reality that existed in heaven.

But at the heart of the legal legislation was the moral law of God that was based on the character of God. Since God is immutable, so are those laws that point to his nature and character. He is truth itself; accordingly, lying is always wrong. God is holy; therefore, we should be as holy as he is. That was the standard then, and it serves as the standard for the present times as well.

The moral law can be found in the Decalogue of Exodus 20 and Deuteronomy 5, as well as in the Holiness Code of Leviticus 18–20.

On the other hand, the book of the covenant (Exod. 21–23) consists mainly of illustrations of God's moral law as seen in the civil laws of the day. The same moral nature of the character and being of God is reflected in the civil laws God enjoined upon the people.

The ceremonial law can be found mainly in Exodus 25–40, Leviticus, and Numbers 1–10. Just as the civil law of the book of the covenant reflects the principles found in the moral law of God, so the ceremonial law reflects those same abiding moral principles.

Illustrating Teaching and Preaching from the Law: Leviticus 16:1–34

Few chapters of the Pentateuch are more important for believers in understanding the nature of the atonement than Leviticus 16. It describes the day that remains to this day as the most holy day in the Jewish calendar: Yom Kippur, or the Day of Atonement. This chapter will serve as our demonstration text from the Torah.

> Sermon/Teaching Title: "God Can Forgive Us of All Our Sin"
> Text: Leviticus 16:1–34
> Homiletical Key Word: Ways
> Interrogative: How? (Can God forgive us of all our sin?)

The law, we often have been told, was a shadow of the things to come. Rarely are we given a more concrete demonstration of doctrinal matters that are abstract in themselves than we find laid out for us in such a concrete and plain manner in Leviticus 16! Moreover, if we admit, as we do, that there is a relationship between the sacrifices ordered here by Moses and Christ's sacrifice for us on the cross, it is important that we determine in what sense the sacrifices of the law took away sin, if at all.

So central is this doctrine of the atonement that many Unitarians spent much labor trying to invalidate it. Unitarians of the 1800s believed that if they could demonstrate that Moses' sacrifices were not involved in any way in removing guilt and obtaining divine pardon, then they would be well on the road to establishing that Christ's death was only an example and not a sin offering for the fallen condition of mankind.

The time set for the Day of Atonement was the tenth day of Tishri, the first month of the civil year (our September-October). It was the only day of fasting commanded by the Torah; however, a number of other fasts were subsequently added by Jewish tradition outside of the biblical corpus.

So let us turn to our text in Leviticus 16 and note the three ways by which God forgave the sin of those early Israelites, for they also supply us with hope and confidence that the same offer remains open even in our day.

By God's Provision of Our Mediator: A Priest (vv. 1–6, 11–14)

The Most Holy Place in the tabernacle was reserved for entrance only on this one day each year, the tenth day of Tishri, the Day of Atonement. Aaron, the high priest, was not to enter this Holy of Holies any time he pleased (v. 2). To do so would be to cause his own death.

In order to help us define the boundaries between the sacred and the common, God set up boundaries. While the boundaries at times may appear to be arbitrary, the point is that God had to be seen as being immanent in this present world and yet also absolutely different from us. He is the Creator; we will always be creatures. He remained holy; we have, since Adam, always been sinners. Thus, in order to prevent a kind of chumminess and flippancy and an unhealthy tearing down of the lines of respect and awe, the boundaries were set for Aaron. By implication, other teachings on holiness in the Torah mark out the same lines for us in our approach to God. There is much to reflect on here with regard to our own worship of God.

The reason for this distance and separation between God and Aaron was that God appeared in the cloud over the atonement seat in the Holy of Holies (v. 2).

But what about this mediator? Will Aaron be adequate for all of us and all subsequent sinners as well? The answer to that is seen in the fact that Aaron's approach to the Holy of Holies must be preceded by a purification of himself. He too is a sinner, and that fact indicates a problem that speaks to the temporary nature of his ability to carry out for all times and all peoples the work that he must now only illustrate. He must offer an expensive bull for himself as a sin offering (v. 3). This is to be followed by the offering of a ram as a whole burnt offering in the dedication of himself and his office to the work he must now carry out to the glory of God.

More than this, he must first bathe himself—the symbol of purification and readiness for service. This is followed by his being clothed with sacred linen garments (v. 4)—undergarments, shirt, shorts, a sash, and a turban—that were set aside especially for this one day of use.

Here is the dramatic point: No longer does he appear in the full panoply of his office of high priest. He must divest himself of that magnificently expensive high priestly robe with its intricate embroidery, its gold, jewels, and colored material. In fact, this picture is so similar to what would happen when our Lord "emptied" himself in Philippians 2:7 and "made himself of no reputation" (KJV) that the similarities cannot be missed. Therefore, as Christ divested himself of what was properly his by way of rights and reputation of his person and office, so Aaron must do in the dress and bearing that he presents on this day.

Again, verse 11 is emphatic: Aaron must "bring the bull for his own sin offering to make atonement for himself and his household, and he is to slaughter the bull for his own sin offering."

It is in this manner that our Lord provides a mediator. Aaron surely shows us most of what is involved, but he carries a major flaw: He too is a sinner. Even though he offers his own sin offering and whole burnt offering, we still long for one who is perfect to be our mediator. This could go on forever unless we get someone who is in himself perfect. But when that one comes who will fulfill this task, he will need to humble himself in order to stoop down and identify with us in our condition. He will need to give up for the moment all the rights, privileges, and powers that go with his person and office. That does not mean that he will be any less divine, as if he, as Charles Wesley ineptly put it, "emptied himself of all but love." That is either high poetry or heresy, for there was more on the cross than just love. He still remained the divine Son of God!

By God's Provision of Our Payment by His Substitutionary Life (vv. 7–10, 15–17, 20–23)

The word that is repeated over and over again is the word *atonement* (vv. 6, 10, 11, 16, 17, 18, 20, 24, 27, 30, 33, 34). This is the translation of the Hebrew word *kipper*. It does not mean, as we have so often taught, "to cover," as if our sins were merely covered by the blood of animals until Christ paid for them. Instead, it means "to ransom or to deliver by a substitute." The picture is clear. Whereas the sinners of Israel's day, like those of our day, were slated for death because of the sins they bore, God boldly provided a substitute that took their place vicariously. In the same manner, the coming Messiah would be that substitute for their sin and ours. This act on the Day of Atonement would point in a concrete way to that coming work of God in Christ.

The propitiatory nature of this sacrifice can be illustrated even more graphically. Two goats were selected by lot to make up this one sin offering (vv. 7–8). Thus, there would be two parts of the one sin offering: (1) sins would be forgiven on the basis of a life that would be substituted for the lives of those who had sinned, and (2) sins would be forgotten and any guilt or blame removed by the second goat that would be sent off into the wilderness, never to return to the camp again. The means of providing for our deliverance would be by the shedding of blood, without which, Scripture teaches, there is no remission. The blood stood for a life that had been surrendered in lieu of our lives—sin was that serious. But the effect was the removal of all guilt from the sinner and from the memory of God. If it be contested that God could not do that since he remains omniscient, we will only retort that God deliberately chooses, as he tells us repeatedly, never to remember our sins against us anymore!

The ceremony proceeded with care. After the two goats had been selected by lot, the first goat was then to be slain on the altar. Its blood was to be carried into the Holy of Holies to be sprinkled on the mercy seat above the ark of the covenant while the smoke of the incense concealed the mercy seat of God in the Holy of Holies. In this way Aaron would not be exposed to the wrath of God by gazing inappropriately on the holy presence of God.

Now that the high priest had returned safely for the second time from the holy presence of God, he was to lay both hands on the head of the live animal and confess *all* the sin of *all* Israel, that is, the sin of all who had grieved in their hearts over their own sin and repented. When this had been done, the live goat was led away by a man specially selected for this job. Since this goat was now bearing the sin of the people, it must be removed from the sight and memory of all who had been forgiven. But

in a similar way God is led away, bearing the iniquities of all
who have called upon him for his deliverance.

Many questions arise. Were the animals symbolic of the people? The imposition of the hands on the head of the goat is con-
clusive on this point (v. 21). All the guilt of the persons forgiven
is borne by the goat in a symbolic transfer of sins from the guilty
to the sin-bearer. Moreover, the goat was considered polluted,
for the man who led the goat away had to bathe and change
clothes before he returned to camp.

Why do some people call the live goat "Azazel"? Does this
mean that they worshiped demons or that the goat was pushed
over a cliff as another sacrifice, as some Jewish authorities
teach? No, it does not; for the Hebrew word *azazel* simply means
"the goat of leading away," or as the Authorized Version put it,
"the scapegoat." The trouble is that in our day a scapegoat is one
who is stuck with doing what others do not wish to do—in other
words the exact reverse of what this text intended and what Old
English had in mind when it first used these words. It simply
signified the goat that was led away and no more.

Sin under the Torah, as under New Testament times, is literally transferred from the sinner to the sin-bearer, that is, to
the one who assumed the load of bearing the offense and thereby
offering the removal of sin from the sinner. Atonement, then,
speaks of the real removal of the guilt and memory of sin.

None of this ceremony was to be automatic or routine. The
rare phrase, "afflict oneself," or as the NIV has it, "deny yourselves" (v. 29), demanded that the Israelites examine themselves
and know what their hearts were like, lest this seem to be a formal ritual that automatically conferred its benefits merely
because the Israelites performed it. This phrase, "to afflict oneself," is repeated in Leviticus 23:27 and 23:32. The prophet Isaiah called for the same inner work of spiritual humiliation and
contrition before God, if Israel was to be forgiven (Isa. 58:3, 5).
The psalmist in another setting said he "put on sackcloth and
humbled [himself] with fasting" (Ps. 35:13).

But what a fantastic provision! The same law, or torah, of
God that demanded the high standard set by the character of
God also provided for all who failed to meet that standard. The
explanation of the two goats and what they did for the people

based on the Word of God also aids our understanding of what God in Christ did on the cross for us as our sin-bearer.

By God's Correspondence between the Day of Atonement and the One Great Expiation the Church Commemorates at Easter (vv. 29–34)

There can be little doubt that the high priest is a type of Christ. Not only is our Lord the victim in the antitype of the sin-offering in its New Testament setting, but he is also the priest who presented the victim. "He offered himself" (Heb. 7:27). And just as the priest had special clothes for this day, so Christ divested himself of the *independent* exercise of his rights and powers as God and took on himself the form of a man; indeed, the form of a bond servant. The high priest trod the winepress alone, for none of his people or his priestly assistants were there to assist or take a portion of the load. He was alone as the Savior of humanity was alone. Thus, men and women are not partners with God in their own deliverance from sin!

Two goats were needed for this illustration even though it was one sin offering. Since the first goat was slain as a substitute for the sins of mortals, a second goat was needed to provide the second half of the illustration. The illustration has some weaknesses, but it is graphic and memorable, and the teaching is secure and great.

Accordingly, we are saved by Christ's death and by his life. This mediatorial work of Christ continues through all the ages in applying the energies of Christ's death and the removal of all guilt, just as it did by the word of the Lord in the illustration found in Moses' day.

There is forgiveness and forgetting of our own sins as illustrated by God's provision for those who failed and sinned under the Torah. The result is that mortals can be pardoned and treated as if they had never offended God, with their sins forgiven and their sins forgotten and remembered against them no more. Therefore, while this message is a word against sin, it is also a proclamation of hope, for in the Savior we too have found the same ransom and deliverance that was first afforded to Israel.

Conclusion

The Torah was not meant to hurt us or to hedge us in so that our options of freedom were drastically reduced. That law gave the guidance we all so desperately needed. But even if Israel failed, as we do, to heed the direction in life that was made available, that same law and grace of God provides forgiveness and a full restoration to our previous relationship with the one we have come to trust and believe in as Lord and Savior.

10

Preaching and Teaching
Old Testament Praise

It had been the custom for teachers and preachers to divide the psalms along the lines of subject, theme, or topic. But Hermann Gunkel[1] (1862–1932) changed that by arguing that the psalms should be grouped according to their function, form, and *Sitz im Leben,* or "setting in life." From that day on, studies in the psalms have begun with a decision as to whether a particular psalm belonged to the category of a lament or a praise form, instead of the old designations based on a topical or subject arrangement.

Here we are concerned mainly with the genre of praise. The two great divisions within the genre of praise are descriptive praise and declarative praise.

Distinguishing Descriptive from Declarative Praise

The key distinction between the two psalm types can be stated succinctly: to recite the attributes or qualities of God is to engage in descriptive praise, but to treat the acts of God is to be involved in declarative praise. Thus, whether the psalmist praised God for who he is (descriptive) or for what he does (declarative), he was praising God.

Since the descriptions of God focus on what he is like and who he is in his nature and being, these psalms fall mainly under the rubric of hymns of praise.

Descriptive psalms include hymns such as Psalms 29, 100, 135–136, and 145–150. The Hebrew verb form of praise is *hillel,* as in the imperative we have brought over into English: "Hallelu-Yah," meaning "praise Yah[weh]," or "praise the LORD."

There are other subcategories of the praise type, including: the enthronement or millennial psalms (47, 93, 95–99); songs of Zion (48, 84, 87); pilgrim psalms sung by those journeying to Jerusalem on the yearly festivals (120–134); and royal psalms (2, 45, 72, 89, 110, 132). All these psalms exhibit three major elements. These elements can be easily illustrated in Psalm 100:

1. A Call to Praise

> Shout for joy to the LORD, all the earth.
> Worship the LORD with gladness;
> come before him with joyful songs.
> Know that the LORD is God (vv. 1–3a).

2. The Cause for Praise (often introduced with Hebrew *ki,* "for" or "because")

It is He who made us, and not we ourselves;
We are His people and the sheep of His pasture (vv. 3b–c NASB).

3. Conclusion or Recapitulation to Praise (often with a repeated call to praise God)

Enter his gates with thanksgiving
   and his courts with praise;
   give thanks to him and praise his name.
For the LORD is good and his love endures forever;
   his faithfulness continues through all generations (vv. 4–5).

Declarative praise, on the other hand, celebrates God for something he has done for the psalmist or the people of God. The most frequent Hebrew verb in these psalms is *hodah,* or *todah*, which is the way to say "thank you" or "thanks" in Israel today. Thus, we are dealing with thanksgiving psalms.

There are only two subcategories of these declarative psalms: individual thanksgiving (Psalms 30, 34, 92, 116, 118, and 138, and Jonah 2) and communal thanksgiving (Psalm 46, 65, 67, and 107).

Just as the descriptive praise psalms have three elements, so the declarative psalms have three main divisions as well. We will use Psalm 34 to illustrate these divisions.

1. An Announcement of What God Has Done (or the Worshiper's Intention to Give Thanks to God)

> I will extol the LORD at all times;
>> his praise will always be on my lips.
> My soul will boast in the LORD;
>> let the afflicted hear and rejoice.
> Glorify the LORD with me;
>> let us exalt his name together (vv. 1–3).

2. The Distress of the Psalmist and His Cry to God for Help

> I sought the LORD, and he answered me;
>> he delivered me from all my fears.
> Those who look to him are radiant;
>> their faces are never covered with shame.
> This poor man called, and the LORD heard him;
>> he saved him out of all his troubles.
> The angel of the LORD encamps around those who fear him,
>> and he delivers them (vv. 4–7).

3. Testifying to God's Help and Prayer for the Future (or Thanksgiving)

> Taste and see that the LORD is good;
>> blessed is the man who takes refuge in him.
> Fear the LORD, you his saints,
>> for those who fear him lack nothing (vv. 8–9).

An Illustration of Teaching and Preaching One of the Praise Psalms: Psalm 84:1–12

One of the songs of Zion is Psalm 84. According to its title, it came from one of the sons of Korah. That in itself is amazing since their ancestor, Korah, perished in the rebellion against Moses and Aaron at the door of the tabernacle (Num. 16). Nevertheless, Korah's descendants were given privileges that left no hint of the stigma that Korah had bequeathed upon his family. How great is the mercy and grace of God, even in the Old Testament! This must be taken into account when we repeat that the judgments of God extend to the third and fourth generation, for too many forget that extension is only for "those who hate me" (Exod. 20:4). However, the mercy and love of God extends for thousands of generations "for those who love me" (v. 6).

Some of Korah's descendants had charge of guarding the temple gates, and others were in charge of the temple music (1 Chron. 9:17–19, 23; 6:33–37; 25:1, 5). Even more striking is the fact that God chose one or more of Korah's descendants to be the agent(s) through which he would send several of the psalms in the Psalter.

Psalm 84 is similar to Psalms 42 and 43. But few of the 150 psalms breathe a more intense spirit of devotion to the Lord than this descriptive praise psalm. This psalm brings us close to God (v. 1); it expresses a yearning and longing for the "living God" (v. 2), makes us feel at home with God (v. 3), and increases our praise and gratitude to God (v. 4). This psalm brings strength to our lives (v. 5), it refreshes us in times of trouble (v. 6), and it revitalizes our strength until we appear before God (v. 7). That meditation describes our praise to God that precedes our prayer to him in verses 8–12. It was Psalm 84:11–12 that my own father wrote across the top of every letter he wrote to me while I was away from home at college in the Midwest. Thus, this psalm of praise also has a special poignancy for me.

It would appear that the speaker of this psalm, God's "anointed" (v. 9), is in some type of calamity, being separated from the sanctuary of the Lord in Zion (vv. 1, 2, 10). Nevertheless, he is resolute in his trust in the Lord.

Such a description would appear to fit the setting of David in flight from his son Absalom, a setting that also fits Psalms 42 and 43. If so, Psalms 42 and 43 would express sadness over being banished, not just from Jerusalem by his usurping son, but from the house of the Lord. Psalm 84, meanwhile, expresses gladness at being able to approach the house of God once again after that ordeal with his son had been concluded. Each of these psalms is at the head of the collection of psalms from the sons of Korah. If this is the proper setting, then the sons of Korah did for David what David once did for Saul—they sang quietness and peace from their souls back to his soul, giving David what they had received from him, their "teacher."[2] Also, the sons of Korah pray for David, for just as they love Yahweh, so they love David, God's "anointed one," who is God's "earnest" or "down payment" on the Messiah who was to come through the line of David.

Sermon/Teaching Title: "Our Longing for an Opportunity to Praise God in His Sanctuary"

Text: Psalm 84:1–12

Focal Point: "Blessed are those who dwell in your house; they are ever praising you" (v. 4).

Interrogative: Why?

Homiletical Key Word: Reasons

Strophe Structure: A threefold blessedness in verses 4, 5, and 12. Thus, the first section (vv. 1–4) ends with a doxology, the second strophe begins with a doxology (v. 5), and the third strophe ends once again with a doxology. This rhetorical device is most helpful in assisting us in marking off the strophe units, which are parallel to the paragraph units in ordinary prose forms. The three major elements of praise are not as pronounced in this psalm as in Psalm 100. However, *the call to praise* does appear in the first strophe of verses 1–4, its *cause for praise* is set out in the second strophe of verses 5–7, and the *conclusion* is marked out in the prayer of the third strophe, verses 8–12.

Because He Is the "Living God" (vv. 1–4)

No phrase is more descriptive of the majesty and might of God than the phrase, "the living God." It occurs about fourteen times each in both the Old[3] and New Testaments. But it signals the most important fact about our Lord: He is alive. He is not an idea or a philosophy but a living person. And the psalmist's soul longs desperately to enter into personal communion with none other than the living God. God himself is the one and only true goal of the worshiper's heart. In fact, the worshiper's whole person, his "soul," his "heart," and his "flesh" cry out with an intensity of desire that knows no rival. True, there is a loveliness to the sanctuary or "dwelling place" of God, just as there is in the "courts of the Lord" (vv. 1, 2). But even though the external place of meeting God is lovely and beautiful beyond description, all of this pales in comparison to the spiritual hunger that the psalmist feels for God himself.

Such an appetite for God's person and being is approved elsewhere in Scripture. For example, in Matthew 5:6 Jesus said, "Blessed are those who hunger and thirst for righteousness, for they will be filled." Accordingly, in proportion to a person's enjoyment of the goodness and graciousness of God, so that person earnestly longs to be more intimately related to the Lord. And as the longing grows for being with the Savior himself, so does that person rejoice in God alone and who he is.

No wonder, then, that all who dwell in the house of God are called "blessed," for "they are ever praising [God]" (v. 4) for who he is and what he has done for them. And should it seem strange that "a place near [God's] altar" should be singled out (v. 3), one need only recall that the altar, rather than the whole house of God, is selected here because at the altar one's relationship to God became possible. Therein lay the grounds for the psalmist's protection and safety. His God was no one less than "O Lord Almighty, my King and my God" (v. 3).

Because He Is Our Strength (vv. 5–7)

After the last strophe closed with a doxology, this next strophe opens immediately with a second doxology (v. 5). The grounds of our joy and praise to God are found in two facts. First, the person who has God for his or her strength knows in his or her heart that there is no other real or lasting comfort than that found in God himself. Second, even though God's people must often pass through bitter experiences, here figuratively called "the Valley of Baca," their sorrow and weeping will be turned into a "place of springs" (v. 6). This is because these same individuals have called on the grace of God by faith. Thus, they go from strength to strength (v. 7; cf. Isa. 40:31). They will see God in Zion once again just as David longed for that prospect after his banishment from the capital by his son Absalom.

BECAUSE HE GRANTS THE BEST GIFTS (VV. 8–12)

Based on what has been said in praise of God, the psalmist enters into prayer in verses 8–12. Three names are used for God in verse 8: "Yahweh," "El Shaddai," and "God of Jacob." The first signifies his constant presence with us, the second his power, which is available to us, and the third his intimate relationship to mortals.

Four verbs set forth the passions of the psalmist in prayer: "hear," "listen," "look," and "look with favor" (v. 8). So what is it that the worshiper wants God to hear and see? It is all that has preceded in verses 1–7. He is saying, "see how hungry I am for you, O God. Nothing will requite my hunger except your very presence and person."

Furthermore, no one but God can be the help and source of safety and security to the believer. Without God's help, both David and we are lost and hopeless. But that is why David is encouraged to turn to God in prayer. He knows that the lowest and most contemptible place in the grace of God is far superior to any lofty place gained by riches, human favor, or wealth (v. 10). One day in God's courts cannot be compared to any other place of eminence or privilege one would ever wish for or experience. So why would anyone want to exchange the joy of being with the living God for residence in the tents of wickedness? He would not! It is better to have the joy of doing little things in the service of God than to experience the painful and bitter end of what looked like pleasure in the tents of wickedness.

But there is a second reason in verse 11. God's favor is the best gift ever given to any mortal. God himself is our "sun and shield." The sun is the source of light and life. Here is where the joy of the natural thirst for God is fulfilled. In the living God there is light and life. On the other hand, God also is our shield, our protection. As far back as the time of Abraham, God had revealed himself as

Abraham's "shield" and his "great reward" (Gen. 15:1). Likewise, Israel had the assurance of Psalm 5:12: "O LORD, you bless the righteous; you surround them with your favor as with a shield."[4]

Both of these metaphors, sun and shield, reflect the beauty of a life lived in the presence of God. The effect that comes from this kind of meditation, communion, and fellowship is a bestowment of "favor and honor" (v. 11). In fact, "no good thing does [God] withhold from those whose walk is blameless." What a promise that is! We ask in surprise, "Not one good thing?" No, not one good thing!

Once more, for the third and last time, we see a doxology. The psalm ends: "Blessed is the man who trusts in you."

So what shall our persuasion be? Can we say with the psalmist that we too desire the presence and person of God more than we long for any other good in life? Do we find that the time spent in the courts of the living God in praise and worship of him is one of the happiest and most desired of all experiences?

Who or what is our sun and shield? And if we desire favor and honor, are we willing to live a lifestyle that is blameless and pure before God? Isn't this what it means to trust in God? May our Lord grant that all that is found in this psalm may be true for each of us to his honor and glory.

Conclusion

Psalms must be our hymnbook of praise, just as it was for Israel.

Whether our praise be descriptive or declarative, such praise must form a part of both our daily expression of affection to God and our preaching and teaching mission to the people of God.

Those who find little about which to praise God are the same ones who find little to praise in the rest of life. Their lives, unfortunately, continue to get narrower and darker as the pressures of life mount. The psalmist can rescue us from our own provincialism and gloominess by giving us a whole new view of the greatness, majesty, and magnificence of God!

11

Preaching and Teaching Old Testament Apocalyptic

The strangest of all the Old Testament genres is the genre of apocalyptic. Above all else, apocalyptic is a specialized form of prophecy that focuses on events surrounding the second coming of Christ and the last things that God will do in history before he ushers in the eternal state. Therefore, in many ways, this genre could be treated as a subcategory of prophecy.

One must not think, however, that apocalyptic is so remote that it bears no contact with the people to whom it was first delivered. On the contrary, few of these future events were so distant that they had no contact with the people of that day when they were first spoken by the prophet, or with people of our own day. Rather, many of these same events participate in what has come to be known as inaugurated eschatology. That is, the future event described in the Scripture frequently has a "now" aspect as well as a "not yet" feature. Just as 1 John 3:2 announced, *"Now* we are children of God, and it has *not* appeared *as yet* what we shall be" (NASB, emphasis added), so prophecy often gives us a present or immediate foretaste of what has not yet come to pass in all its fullness. That is why 1 John 2:18 warns that "the antichrist is coming, [but] even now many antichrists have come" already! One must not despair if his or her candidate for the office of antichrist vacated the scene without our seeing the second coming of Christ; it may have been only one in a long line of many that will precede the final antichrist.

The Meaning of Apocalyptic

The name for this genre comes from the title of the Book of Revelation, which in Greek is *apokalypsis,* a "revelation." Accordingly, the form is not as sharp as some have claimed,[1] for it does not exhibit its own special format and literary shape in the scriptural text. We are usually given topical, subject, and theme descriptions for this genre rather than any distinctive forms or formats in the text itself.

If the method assumes that our first task is to try to link earlier Old Testament images, symbols, and dreams with the Book of Revelation and then to extrapolate backward into the intertestamental period to apocalyptic books, we must be as critical of such a procedure as we are of eisegesis, or reading a meaning back into a text. For many, study in books such as 1 Enoch or the Dead Sea War Scroll involves a process of reading similar themes found in the New Testament back into the intertestamental books and then incorporating those "results" as a basis for reading the apocalyptic materials of the Old Testament. A similar process is sometimes used for the books of the Old Testament, where the intertestamental meanings of apocryphal books are read back into the Old Testament, but there the stretch is a forward one that tends to retroject that meaning back on the older text. This too is eisegesis. It tends to confuse and summarily equate the symbols and images of the later Jewish religion of the exile and the postexilic period with the divine disclosures made in the earlier parts of the Old Testament. But it is incorrect to equate these two epochs of writing and thinking or to make them identical—at least, to do so without warrant from the text itself.

This same process has also been used as a lever by the critical school to late-date the designated apocalyptic materials in Daniel 7–12, Isaiah 58–66, and Zechariah 12–14, placing them considerably later in time than the texts themselves claim to have been written. But this late-dating is only as secure as the criteria that has been raised *ex post facto.*

Also, apocalypses from the ancient world often are pseudonymous. This leads many to suggest that perhaps the portions of the prophets' works that deal with apocalyptic topics, especially the latter half of the Book of Daniel and the sections of Isaiah and Zechariah listed above, are likewise pseudonymous. But here again the wish is parent to the thought, for the only evidence to support the fact that these sections come from unknown authors is the bias found in the definition itself. Priority ought to be given to asking the text itself about its claim concerning authorship. Only then can a decision be rendered whether the claims are reliable or not.

Since apocalyptic is a subcategory of prophecy, it should be treated in many ways as one would treat the genre of prophecy. In many instances, the message about a glorious or cataclysmic future is given as a conclusion to a threatened word of judgment or to a message of ultimate salvation. The point is this: God is not willing to let the judgment that must come in the present order of Israel's life (or any other nation for that matter) be his final word. It should not be taken to indicate that his promise-plan has now been averted or, worse still, ruined. The listener is therefore taken far beyond the days of the prophet to hear how God will deal with all evil or how he will magnificently triumph in his own glory.

It is not as though the immediate future and the distant future have nothing to do with each other. On the contrary, often there is a direct connection in the form of the immediate future being an earnest, or a down payment, on the distant future.

A good place to show this connection between the now and the not yet is in the prophecy of Joel. A fourfold (or four-waved) locust plague had come because of the people's slowness to turn back to God. Finally, after two calls for repentance by the prophet Joel (Joel 1:13–14; 2:12–14), Israel turned sharply around.

The proof of genuine repentance of heart by Joel's listeners can be found in the four past tense verbs in Joel 2:18–19 (contrary to the impossible future rendering given to the same four verbs in the NASB and the NIV[2]), which declares:

> The LORD was jealous for his land,
> and he took pity on his people;
> the LORD answered
> and the LORD said to them . . . (my translation)

The only way God could have responded so graciously was if the people finally, in the desperation and destitution caused by the locust invasions and the resulting drought, genuinely repented as the prophet had begged them to do prior to these infestations. As a result, two marvelous gifts of God were promised. First, new showers would immediately come on the land and cause its pastures to turn green and the land to become productive again (Joel 2:19b–27). Second, a downpour (not just a shower) of the Holy Spirit would come in the distant future, followed much later (apparently) by a cosmic shake-up in that great and dreadful day of the Lord (Joel 2:28–3:21).

Analyzing the Constituent Parts of Apocalyptic

A suggested model for analyzing an apocalyptic portion of the Old Testament can be seen in Joel 3:1–21, which has these five typical elements:

1. An Announcement about the Last Days

> In those days and at that time,
>   when I restore the fortunes of Judah and Jerusalem,
> I will gather all nations
>   and bring them down to the Valley of Jehoshaphat.
> There I will enter into judgment against them
>   concerning my inheritance, my people Israel (vv. 1–2a).

2. An Explanation and a Reason for This Announced Action

> For they scattered my people among the nations
>   and divided up my land.
> They cast lots for my people. . . .
> [They] took my silver and my gold
>   and carried off my finest treasures to your temples
>   (vv. 2b–3a, 5).

3. A Declaration of War on Evil and a Summons for the Enemies of God to Present Themselves for Earth's Final Showdown

Proclaim this among the nations: Prepare for war!
   Rouse the warriors! Let all the fighting men draw near
     and attack.
Beat your plowshares into swords
   and your pruning hooks into spears.
Let the weakling say, "I am strong!"
Come quickly, all you nations from every side,
   and assemble there.
Bring down your warriors, O LORD!
"Let the nations be roused;
   Let them advance into the Valley of Jehoshaphat,
for there I will sit to judge all the nations on every side" (vv.
9–12).

4. The Horrors of the Day of the LORD Described

"Swing the sickle,
   for the harvest is ripe.
Come, trample the grapes,
   for the winepress is full
   and the vats overflow—
so great is their wickedness!"
Multitudes, multitudes
   in the valley of decision!
For the day of the LORD is near
   in the valley of decision.
The sun and moon will be darkened,
   and the stars no longer shine.
The LORD will roar from Zion
   and thunder from Jerusalem;
   the earth and the sky will tremble.
But the LORD will be a refuge for his people,
   a stronghold for the people of Israel (vv. 13–16).

5. A Listing of the Final Blessings of the LORD for His People

"Then you will know that I, the LORD your God,
dwell in Zion, my holy hill.
Jerusalem will be holy;
   never again will foreigners invade her.
In that day the mountains will drip new wine,
   and the hills will flow with milk;

all the ravines of Judah will run with water.
A fountain will flow out of the Lord's house
and will water the valley of acacias.
But Egypt will be desolate,
Edom a desert waste,
because of the violence done to the people of Judah,
in whose land they shed innocent blood.
Judah will be inhabited forever
and Jerusalem through all generations.
Their bloodguilt, which I have not pardoned,
I will pardon."
The Lord dwells in Zion! (vv. 17–21).

An Illustration on How to Preach Old Testament Apocalyptic: Daniel 9:20–27

The passage I have chosen is both apocalyptic and at the heart of many eschatological debates. The focal point for the passage is Daniel 9:24: "Seventy 'sevens' are decreed for your people and your holy city to finish transgression, to put an end to sin, to atone for wickedness, to bring in everlasting righteousness, to seal up vision and prophecy and to anoint the most holy [One or place]." The title of our message, then, will be "Announcing God's Program to Wrap Up History."

The immediate context features one of the great intercessory prayers of the Bible. Daniel has noticed in his reading of the Scriptures, which were given "according to the word of the Lord . . . to Jeremiah the prophet" (Dan. 9:2; cf. Jer. 25:12–14; 29:10–14), that the seventy years of exile are about to be finished. His question is whether God would forgive the sins of all Israel and once again look with favor on the city of Jerusalem and the people of Israel.

Notice that Jeremiah's prophecy is called Scripture, yet the ink is hardly dry, for Jeremiah gave his seventy-year prophecies in the first year of Nebuchadnezzar (605 B.C.; Jer. 25:1). It is now the first year of King Darius, the son of Xerxes (539 B.C.)—a mere sixty-five years later! Daniel did not need to wait for any Council of Jamnia (A.D. 90) to help him decide whether Jeremiah was in the canon or not. He already regarded Jeremiah's writings as Scripture.

The angel Gabriel (Dan. 9:21) was sent while Daniel was still in prayer. He had come to give Daniel "insight and understanding" (v. 22), for God found Daniel "highly esteemed" (v. 23) and therefore wanted to answer his prayers.

Let us examine the structure of Daniel 9:24–27 first, for the actual apocalyptic message begins in verse 24.

I. An Announcement about the Last Days: "Seventy 'sevens' are decreed for your people and your holy city" (plus six purpose statements or infinitives, v. 24).

II. An Explanation or Reason for This Announcement: "Know and understand this: From the issuing of the decree to restore and rebuild Jerusalem until the Anointed One, the ruler, comes, there will be seven 'sevens,' and sixty-two 'sevens.'" (vv. 25–26a).

III. The Horrors of That Day Described: "War will continue until the end, and desolations have been decreed. . . ." (vv. 26b–27).

Sermon/Teaching Title: "Announcing God's Program to Wrap Up History"

Text: Daniel 9:24–27

Homiletical Key Word: Blocks (of time in the program of God)

Interrogative: What? (What are the blocks of time in the program?)

I. God Will Give Us One More Set of Seventies to Complete History (v. 24)
  A. Seventy More "Sevens" after the Seventy-Year Captivity
    1. For the people of Israel—"Your people"
    2. For the holy city of Jerusalem—"Your holy city"
  B. Purpose of these Seventy "Sevens"
    1. To finish transgression
    2. To put an end to sin
    3. To atone for wickedness
    4. To bring in everlasting righteousness
    5. To seal up vision and prophecy
    6. To anoint the most holy [One or place]

II. God Will Explain to Us in Understandable Terms This Program for the Future (vv. 25–26a)
   A. The Signal for the End to Begin
      1. The issuing of a decree. But which one?
         a. Cyrus's decree in 536 B.C.?
         b. Ezra's decree in 557 B.C.?
         c. Nehemiah's decree in 445 B.C.?
      2. Reasons for deciding on Nehemiah's decree
   B. The Remaining History Is Set into Three Sets of "Sevens" or Years
      1. Seven "sevens" (or forty-nine years) are for Jerusalem to be rebuilt and restored
      2. Sixty-two additional "sevens" will be until Messiah, the ruler/prince, comes
   C. The Break in the Program of God
      1. "After" the first sixty-nine "sevens," two events will take place
         a. Messiah, the "Anointed One" will be "cut off"—Christ's death on the cross c. A.D. 30
         b. The city and the sanctuary will be destroyed—in A.D. 70
      2. Then the end will come like a flood
III. God Will Oversee the Wrap-up of History (vv. 26b–27)
   A. "War Will Continue until the End"
   B. One Will Make a Covenant with Many for the Last "Seven"
      1. In the middle of the last "seven" years, this one will do the following:
         a. End sacrifices and offerings
         b. Set up an abomination that causes desolation
      2. The decreed end will be poured out on this one

This text is an answer to Daniel's prayer after he had finished reading what we now know as Jeremiah 29:10–14 and Jeremiah 25:12–14. Indeed, the seventy years mentioned in the revelation of God to the prophet had almost expired. So what would God do now?

It is foolish to insert a symbolic explanation for the natural one that the angel Gabriel gave in this text. The prophecy was to show Daniel what would happen to Israel, his people, and to the holy city, Jerusalem. It was not given primarily to show what would happen to the Gentiles or the church. Furthermore, we must receive this prophecy today in the mood of prayer, as Daniel did, and not in a cold or merely intellectual way.

GOD WILL GIVE US ONE MORE SET OF SEVENTIES TO COMPLETE HISTORY (v. 24)

The program of God would involve another set of "seventy sevens," or "seventy weeks," beyond the seventy years that were just being accomplished. This new set of "seventy sevens" would be divided into three distinct blocks: one set of "seven weeks," another of "sixty-two sevens" (or "weeks"), and a final "seven."

It is clear from Daniel's use of "sevens," or "weeks," that he intends them to be understood as years, for in Daniel 4:16, 23, and 25, Daniel predicts that "seven times" are to pass over Nebuchadnezzar until he repents of his proud ways. This turns out to be seven years. The same could be said for Daniel 4:25 and 32.

The purpose for these 490 years is found in the sixfold statement that follows. First, these years were necessary "to finish transgression." In other words, to push back or lock up transgression and sin of all mortals by bringing an end to the long series of apostasies, uprisings against God, and sinful rebellion against his law and will. Parallel to this was the second purpose: "to make an end of sin" (NASB). Third, it was "to make reconciliation for iniquity" (NKJV). Here is an allusion to the mercy of God as he in Christ atoned for Israel's sin. Fourth, these years were needed "to bring in everlasting righteousness." Such final justice and right standing before God could only be possible by Christ's death. Fifth, at the end of those days, the "vision and prophecy" would be sealed up. That is, all prediction about Israel and the temple would be completed as this period came to an end. Finally, it was "to anoint the most holy [One or place]." Since this expression is never used of a person, it probably is not a reference to the Messiah or even to his church. Rather, it is the bliss and holiness that will be conferred on everything that will be holy to the Lord (Zech. 14:20).

God Will Explain to Us in Understandable Terms This Program for the Future (vv. 25–26b)

This message was not meant to be an encoded message with an esoteric meaning open only to a privileged few. Daniel wanted all of us to "know and understand." The decree, or "command," went forth in Nehemiah's term in Jerusalem in 445 B.C. The seven weeks of this period ended after 49 years.

A second set of sixty-two weeks, or 434 years, takes us up to the time of Messiah. Even though these were to be troublesome times, the ending would bring the Messiah himself.

The most critical part of this apocalyptic message comes in verse 26. It says, "And after the sixty-two weeks Messiah shall be cut off, . . . and the people of the prince . . . shall destroy the city and the sanctuary" (NKJV). These references can be nothing other than allusions to the death of Christ in A.D. 30 and the fall of Jerusalem in A.D. 70. This means that the sequence of the seventy weeks has been interrupted, with a gap now existing between the end of the sixty-ninth week (which resulted in the arrival of Messiah's first advent) and the start of the seventieth week (an event that many understand as not having happened yet).

The "prince who is to come" (NKJV) seems to be a reference first to the Roman ruler Vespasian or Titus (the "now" part of the inaugurated eschatology), and also to the Antichrist (the "not yet" part of that same inaugurated eschatological view; see v. 27). This, as we have said, is in keeping with an inaugurated eschatology in which the near and the distant future are blended together in a single meaning, even though it has multiple fulfillments. As such, the two Roman generals who were responsible for the destruction of the city of Jerusalem and the burning of the temple were also types of the final person who will come to Jerusalem and make his ultimate assault on the city and the kingdom of God.

Even though the Messiah is crucified, it will "not [be] for himself" (NKJV). That is, he will have nothing personally to gain from this experience: no glory, no adulation, or even appreciation from the people.

God Will Oversee the Wrap-up of History (vv. 26c–27)

"The end will come like a flood." Wars will continue up to the very end, but the climax to history will come like a dam breaking loose.

The prince who was to come will oppose God by oppressing Israel. In order to work his will, Antichrist will "confirm a covenant with many for one week" (NKJV), a seven-year period. The text does not indicate whether this begins as an open or secret covenant. In the middle of this period, however, the Antichrist will break this covenant with Israel. This will involve Antichrist's taking off his mask, as it were. Then he will suddenly turn on Israel with almost demonic fury. Sacrifices in the temple will be stopped; instead, Antichrist will set himself up in the temple and pretend to be God.

What the precise nature of the "abomination that causes desolation" is cannot be determined with any finality; however, our Lord alluded to this event in Matthew 24:15. When this happens, our Lord advised, let the reader flee Judea to the mountains.

Even though this is an apocalyptic text, we are not to think that it is mysterious and not understandable. Even our Lord said that all who read this text were to understand (Matt. 24:15). Moreover, the crucifixion of Messiah and the fall of Jerusalem were not unknown to our Lord, for they were all in his eternal plan. But it is the six purposes of these days that bring comfort to us in our day. Sin will have ended by the time this is all over. Moreover, everlasting righteousness will be introduced and will never end. What a revelation this is to keep our hearts, minds, and eyes fixed on our Savior and not merely on the signs of the times. He has told us about these things before they happen so that when they do take place, we may recognize that God has been faithful and he is sovereign over all times and persons. This is much to be preferred to our arguing that our time chart was correct or that we knew ahead of time. Thanks be to God for his plan, his death, and his triumph over all sin, death, and evil!

Conclusion

Old Testament apocalyptic is a strange genre, to say the least. It has fewer textual markers than other genres and depends more on its high use of figurative language that is anchored in events, terms, and citations from previously written Scripture rather than importing later revelation to unlock its use of terms or symbols. This means that in order to interpret this genre, one must look at past Scriptures to gain an appreciation for what is being said. This method also shares great similarities with the method known as the analogy of antecedent Scripture.[3]

However, all the other parts of preparing an apocalyptic text of Scripture for teaching or preaching will be much the same as for developing texts from other portions of the prophets.

Conclusion

Changing the World
with the Word of God

"But the word of the Lord continued to grow and to be multiplied."

Acts 12:24 NASB

"And the word of the Lord was being spread through the whole region."

Acts 13:49 NASB

"So the word of the Lord was growing mightily and prevailing."

Acts 19:20 NASB

When all is said and done, the Book of Acts offers us the best picture of what the believing body was meant to be. Acts 2:42 describes a congregation that was "continually devoting themselves to the apostles' teaching" (NASB). Acts also notes that "the word of God kept on spreading; and the number of disciples continued to increase greatly" (6:7 NASB).

But how could that first-century group of believers have been so successful when we in the twenty-first century have tried almost every trick in the bag only to come up short of the powerful demonstration of the working of the Holy Spirit that we see in the Book of Acts? If the Word of God is supposed to be all that powerful, why is it that even some of the strongest saints of God in our day seem to balk at anything beyond baby steps in the Christian faith and biblical teaching?

173

Yet, we cannot mistake the fact that the Word of God must be the hallmark of any powerful manifestation of the Holy Spirit in our midst. It must be stated with all the passion of our souls that in the seven summaries of the fantastic growth of the church in the Book of Acts (6:7; 9:31; 12:24; 13:49; 16:5; 19:20; 28:31), five of the seven connect this growth directly to the preaching of the Word of God. Even in the two indirect cases (9:31 and 16:5), it is still the word found in the Scriptures that builds the body and sponsors the growth that takes place.

So let us mark it down as a principle: Where the preaching of God's Word is thin or abandoned for more "relevant" issues and encouragements, the growth, power, and effectiveness of the church wanes and ultimately is extinguished. But where the Word of God multiplies, spreads, and is sought after by all, the body of Christ demonstrates a resourcefulness and a power that goes forward despite all modern or ancient barriers, oppositions, or persecutions.

Some will object, of course, that biblical preaching is often too dull, boring, insipid, bland, anemic, and without contemporary relevance to be of any use in the twenty-first century. Such objections contend that it is meaningless to have people sit in rows as spectators soaking up dry, dusty tracings of God's workings in the history of Israel and the early church. But if this has been our experience (and who can deny that it does fit at least some of our churches), then it does not match what the Book of Acts describes or what God has intended for us. What has straw to do with real grain? It may look like biblical preaching, act like it, and even make a passing reference or two to the Bible, but it is not the powerful demonstration of the Holy Spirit joined to a fair presentation of the Word of God in preaching, which proceeds paragraph after paragraph and chapter after chapter in an effort to announce the whole counsel of God.

What is called for is not a rote bag of wind that is pirated from some self-help book or someone's four or five easy steps to be this or that in life! The Book of Acts gives us precedence to expect that where the Word of God is preached faithfully—both in its replication of the exact content of the passage and in its structure—there we can expect to see the power of the Holy Spirit joining the Word of God and having a profound effect not only on the speaker, but on the hearer as well. Not every message or any kind of preaching will cut through the barriers of our anti-Christian and postmodern culture. Only diligent exposition of the text under the mighty hand of God's Holy Spirit will fill the vacuum of our day. And that exposition must read the context and the culture into which that message is delivered with as much accuracy as it reads the text itself. The expositor and teacher must know the contemporary idiom as well as the biblical idiom. Both substance and form deserve our best efforts under the mighty hand of the Holy Spirit.

Authority for an Individualistic Society

The blessing and the curse of life in the West is our emphasis on individualism. The bad part of this emphasis is that we forget we are part of a larger group as we stand as individuals before God. Our tendency is to say that we have no responsibility for the group and that what happens to my nation, my city, my church, or the rest of my family is not any of my concern or responsibility.

Scripture will not let us off the hook so easily. Scripture asserts that I indeed am my brother's keeper. I am part of a culture and a nation that is fast approaching the judgment of God for its refusal to acknowledge him and obey his law and his commands. Just as we all benefit when those who preceded us lived righteous and holy lives, because the dividends passed down to our generation, so we all stand to lose or gain when the group we belong to nationally, denominationally, or filially turns its back on God or in repentance dramatically turns back to God for forgiveness.

But where can we turn if the prevailing thought affirms the new principle of postmodernism that "I can do whatever I wish to do as long as I judge that it doesn't hurt anyone else"?

Here is individualism gone to seed. It seems to assume that we can be our own authorities and our own judges for everything—including faith and morals.

But that is just where we need to have the corrective of the powerful preaching of God's Word once again. All authority emanates from our Lord and his Word. If he is not the final arbiter and source of authority, then how can we stop short of anarchy—where everyone is his or her own chief judge, jury, and prosecutor?

That's the whole point of what I have labored to show in this book. We must go back to the testimonies and standards of Scripture for the authority lost in our generation, or we are sunk and without any guide in our culture.

Proverbs 29:18 asserts, "Where there is no vision, the people perish" (KJV). The word for "vision" did not refer to a five- or ten-year plan, as we have often applied this text. No, it meant a "revelation" of the word of God. Thus, this verse claims that given the absence of any input of the revelatory word of God, the populace in general will go mad and run wild. As we have seen, the word used by the writer of Proverbs for "perish" had a historical past. It is found in Exodus 32:25, where it says that the people of Israel were "running wild" casting off all restraint as they shed their clothes and went into religious prostitution around the golden calf, much to the horror of Moses as he descended from the mount. Is that not a vivid picture of our own day? Left to ourselves without the faithful and careful exposition of Scripture, have we not often watched as both the church and culture continue to go mad and expose themselves to devastating destruction? Moses was gone for less than six weeks. Did Aaron fail to proclaim the word of God for even that short period of time, thus contributing to the devastating erosion of all that had been placed before the people of God prior to that time?

The point is that we do not live by our wits, our intelligence, our grandchildren, or even our degrees; we do live, however, by every word that proceeds from the mouth of God. That is the only source of authority and health for the body of Christ. All else leads to the shambles we are seeing in many quarters today. Praise God for the wonderful exceptions, but these preachers who are trying to be faithful to the Word of God are facing an uphill battle against many who have drunk heavily of the waters of modernity and postmodernity.

Application in a Pluralistic Society

It will be of little use to anyone in our day if the Bible is proven to be authoritative but not applicable to any of our issues. In fact, our present flirtation with pluralism stresses the legitimacy of everyone being right at the same time, while holding contradictory conclusions on the same subjects. Thus, if we approach Scripture with the same rules, then Scripture will have as many meanings as there are people. And when the Bible can mean anything to anyone, even if all the views contradict one another, then it ultimately means nothing!

How, then, shall we apply the Scriptures in a way that will demonstrate their contemporary significance without falling into the modern trap of pluralism? Shall we extract a relevant application of an ancient text at the expense of losing its authority or being fair to the original assertions and intentions of the author? Of course not!

Application of Scripture calls for the fine art of retaining the truth of what the text *meant* while also moving to those legitimate illustrations of what that same text *means* in the new situations of our day. Proper application of a text bears out the same principles argued for in its original setting. The particularity of the text in its ancient setting was not meant to keep us from applying that text to contemporary situations; instead, it was meant to illustrate for us how a principle was also applied in another day and time. Such applications for the past give us more than just vague hints as to how we can apply such texts in our own day.

We seem to have less trouble making this transition of applying the text to a contemporary situation when dealing with the New Testament. For example, in Philippians 4:2 the apostle Paul was pleading with "Euodia and . . . Syntyche to agree with each other in the Lord." Now few, if any, merely wave their hands and say, "Since I am not Euodia or Syntyche, I am not going to bother with that little historical bit of gossip." Rather, most say, "These two women had some sort of disagreement that must have been upsetting the church at Philippi. The application for us must be that we 'Be kind and compassionate to one another, forgiving each other, just as in Christ God [has forgiven us]'" (Eph. 4:32).

Exactly. That is how we should likewise handle the Old Testament, even though it is farther removed from us and from our times.

A New Call for Preaching the Old Testament

With over three-fourths of God's revelation at stake, there must be a whole new breed of proclaimers of the Word of God who will announce the whole counsel of God (Acts 20:27 NKJV) to a hungry and waiting generation. It is my observation that we are generally in the midst of one of the most starved generations for the hearing of the Word of God. Amos 8:11–12 warned of days when there would be a hunger, not just for bread and water, but for the hearing of the words of God. There are large portions of Scripture that have never been announced to some of God's sheep, and they are malnourished because of it.

One of my teachers observed in class one day that if we leave any portion of God's Word unattended and without exposition, it will become a potential seedbed for heresy in the next generation. My teacher, Dr. Merrill Tenney, is now with the Lord, but I do not think he would mind if I also added that in the mercy of God, he has often sent a parachurch ministry to fill the gaps the church has left in the hearts and minds of those who should have been ministered to more fully and completely. For example, marriage enrichment seminars have taught the long-neglected Song of Songs and youth conflict seminars have taught the neglected Book of Proverbs.

In the days of Samuel, the word of God was "scarce" and "rare," because God had hidden his teachers after a rebellious generation had refused to repent or listen to God's message. Will we need to fall into that same trap before we come to our senses and realize how starved we really are? I hope not.

Let the Word of God be proclaimed with all of its authority, power, and winsomeness. The Holy Spirit will show us once again what it means to have the mighty Word of God joined by the convincing and convicting power of the Holy Spirit to change a people, a nation, and a church that has, for the most part, failed to preach the whole counsel of God to a waiting generation.

Let us teach the whole counsel of God with a joy and passion that comes from above. And may times of refreshing and revival break out all over the land once again to the glory of God.

Appendix A

Suggested Worksheet for Doing Syntactical-Theological Exegesis

The principles and practices I suggest as being the most helpful have been stated in greater detail in the preceding chapters of this book. They are also set forth in the volume *Toward an Exegetical Theology: Biblical Exegesis for Preaching and Teaching.* Rather than laying down these features again, I will merely follow the outline found in part 2 of *Toward an Exegetical Theology.* These steps will help each student of the Scriptures, whether preparing a lesson for a Bible study group, writing a college or seminary exegesis paper, preparing a Sunday school lesson, studying in one's own private devotions, or producing a sermon for Sunday morning. Obviously, you may want to make modifications to fit your own style and emphasis; however, my argument is that without the following components, the chances for that preparation to fall stillborn on the ears of its hearers is extremely high since it will usually fail to exhibit the ring of authority that is found in the text.

The process I advocate here and in *Toward an Exegetical Theology* includes five basic steps in preparing a text for preaching or teaching:

1. Contextual analysis
2. Syntactical analysis
3. Verbal analysis
4. Theological analysis
5. Homiletical analysis

In order to give definite form to what would otherwise be an overwhelming task, I advise that for each lesson, sermon, or study attempted, the expositor or teacher devote about seven or eight full-size pages of paper to each biblical passage selected. These pages should follow the approximate layout outlined below.

Contextual Analysis (page 1)

Every passage of Scripture has three basic contexts: (1) a canonical context, (2) a book and section-of-the-book context, and (3) an immediate context. Contexts are important, for they help us to see the forest before we focus on the trees.

Canonical Context

Before attempting to speak, teach, or learn from any individual passage selected for exposition or teaching, some understanding of the whole plan of God found in the whole Bible is necessary. This may be achieved by reading the Bible through several times and asking, "If the Bible is the work of one mind, namely the mind of God, what is the central idea or the plan that unifies the whole of the Scriptures?"

Another way to achieve this is to study Old and New Testament biblical theologies. In the Old Testament, I suggest a work that I did some years ago, titled *Toward an Old Testament Theology*. In that volume, I argued that there is a single promise-plan of God, which was given most explicitly to Abraham at first but was intended to be God's declaration of the means whereby he would bless the whole world. Another such volume came from the pen of Elmer A. Martens in 1981, *God's Design: A Focus on Old Testament Theology*.

Book and Section Context

After we have described in a sentence or two the unifying theme of the whole Bible, it is time to ask two other questions: (1) What is the overall purpose and plan for the book of the Bible in which our passage is found? And, (2) where are the natural breaks that form the major sections of that book of the Bible and that carry out that book's plan and purpose?

For example, in the book of Malachi, I would suggest that the overall purpose and plan can be found in two texts:

"I have loved you, says the LORD" (1:2).
"I the LORD do not change" (3:6).

Thus, I would propose that the purpose of Malachi is to reveal God's unchanging love to us.

The divisions of the book are important if we wish to see how the plan and purpose unfold. Sometimes there are repeated words or formulas that come at the beginning (rubrics) or at the end (colophons) of each section, thereby allowing us to see the author's own way of sectioning the text for us. Malachi uses the device of a question from the audience to introduce each of his six sections in the book (1:1–5; 1:6–2:9; 2:10–16; 2:17–3:6; 3:7–12; 3:13–4:6). Other sections are set off by colophons, such as Isaiah 40–48, Isaiah 49–57, and Isaiah 58–66, with the phrase coming at the end of the first two: "There is no peace . . . for the wicked" (48:22; 57:21).

Immediate Context

Identify in a short paragraph or two what has preceded and what follows the block of text that is to be taught. This context has a historical, geographical, and literary setting. Here one should rely on Bible dictionaries, Bible encyclopedias, archaeology journals, histories of Israel, and the like.

The question that must be answered here is how this text contributes to the whole purpose of the book and section in which it is found. Then we must assess what new contribution to that overall strategy is found in this teaching block that has been selected.

Syntactical Analysis (pages 2–3)

Literary Type

Each portion of the Bible has its own distinctive literary format that belongs to one of the genres treated in the previous chapters. With the descriptions given in these chapters, we must locate the proper genre and then proceed to interpret it in accordance with the demands of that literary type.

Paragraphing and Its Related Forms

In prose passages, our text will show its development with the use of paragraphs. A paragraph is simply a unit of thought that generally contains a single idea. In a poetic genre, the equivalent designators for the advancement of single ideas will be strophes. A narrative passage, on the other hand, will employ scenes to advance its thought.

The best way to determine these paragraphs, strophes, or scenes is to first attempt to see where the idea changes. After you have made an initial division of the texts into paragraphs, strophes, or scenes, consult four or five English or Hebrew versions of the same texts to see what agreements or disagreements there are.

I would urge making a simple grid that lists the abbreviations for the various versions consulted (such as KJV, RSV, NASB, NIV, NEB, or NAB) at the top of a sheet of paper. Then list down the left-hand margin the numbering of the verses in your passage. Then draw a horizontal line at the number of each verse where each version ends its paragraph (or its equivalent). A final column could be labeled "My Own" to show your final decision for where the paragraphing should come with a list of reasons briefly stated at the bottom of the sheet.

Note that each scene usually is marked off where there is a change of time, place, or persons. It is true that many versions (such as the NIV) mark a change whenever there is a change of speaker, but this leads to a situation where one has too many points for the purpose of preaching. Also, the various speakers often are still in the same place or dealing with the same situation, so there is no need for the interpreter to introduce a new thought or principal point in his or her outline.

Topic Sentence

After you have marked off the paragraphs (or their equivalents in other genres), the next step is to identify the theme or topic sentence in each paragraph. This sentence may come at the beginning, middle, or end of the paragraph. Almost always it is expressed and represents the key idea that tells what the paragraph is all about.

Block Diagramming or a Mechanical Layout of the Passage

Once you have found the topic sentence for each paragraph, it is best to take an unlined piece of paper and draw a one-inch margin on the left-hand side of the paper (or right-hand side of the sheet if you are going to do it in Hebrew, since Hebrew is written from right to left).

Place the topic sentence all the way out to the margin that you have just drawn. Then, show how each clause, phrase, and sentence is related to that theme sentence by indenting the clause, phrase, or sentence to fit under (if it follows the theme/topic sentence in the paragraph) or above it (if it precedes the topic sentence). Grammar and syntax are the true determiners of where to place the indentation, with an arrow pointing to the word that the clause or phrase modifies or is related to grammatically. Every time a punctuation mark (a comma, semicolon, period, question mark, exclamation point) appears or a phrase or clause ends, we must make a decision: "Which way did the action go?" It is similar to driving and coming to an intersection in the roadway: Should we go straight across the intersection or should we turn right or left? That is the decision the exegete also must make.

It is the discipline of being forced to face such decisions about these grammatical and syntactical features that slow us down enough to make sure we really are listening to what is being taught, described, or held up for our learning and growth in the Scriptures.

Verbal Analysis (page 4)

The question often is asked, "What words should I pay attention to in the text?" The first answer to that question is that I must study all the words that give me trouble and that I do not know. These often are the best words to focus on since they are the points where I can learn and grow myself. If I as a preacher and teacher am not growing, then it is certain that my congregation or students are not growing either. Water can rise only as high as its source. The same is true in this case.

We must also be aware that the Bible is a rich source of figurative expressions. It is best to consult E. W. Bullinger's *Figures of Speech Used in the Bible*. This work, which first appeared in 1898 and has more recently been reprinted by Baker Books, is a wonderful source for some 250 different figures of speech with some 8,000 illustrations from the Bible. Its index with each passage of the Bible listed in canonical order by book, chapter, and verse, is as great an interpreter's sourcebook as one can find anywhere.

Theological Analysis (pages 5–6)

One particular type of verbal analysis must be lifted from its category to receive special attention because of its technical importance and the depth that it adds to our teaching and preaching. This is the study of all the theological concepts that are found in a passage.

Many theological words may not be spotted immediately by the beginner, but the more one reads the Bible, the more one is alert to these terms and concepts as they appear in the various texts.

The four ways we can get at these ideas are through (1) key theological terms that have taken on technical status because of the frequency of their usage or their first appearance in pivotal passages, (2) the analogy of antecedent Scripture, (3) the analogy of faith, and (4) commentaries. Each of these four ways needs to be explained further.

Key Theological Terms

One may depend either on his or her own Bible knowledge or on the use of chain-reference Bibles like the *Dickson Chain*

Reference Bible or the *Thompson Chain Reference Bible.* Other printed editions of the Bible often include marginal cross-references to other places where the same terms and theological concepts appear. Most study Bibles offer the same help. On a purely topical basis, one could check a source such as *Nave's Topical Study Bible.* Others will want to use the table of contents or the indexes of biblical theologies or even more importantly the numerous theological wordbooks and theological dictionaries in English, Hebrew, and Greek.

Many of these lexical studies are divided into four parts: (1) descriptive aspects (covering matters of form and function), (2) distribution studies (how many times a word is used in each of its grammatical forms and in which books), (3) cognates and comparisons with words in other Semitic languages, and (4) contextual aspects of the word.

The Analogy of Antecedent Scripture

Many theological terms have an "inner history of exegesis." That is, the very same terms were used in one or more key passages that appeared earlier than the text under consideration. In most of these cases, the later writer was using this earlier term with the understanding that it had gathered from its first appearance, for in his time that earlier writing was the Bible against which the later writer heard this new word from God.

These references could be in the form of identical theological terms, allusions or direct citations from earlier texts, or allusions and direct references to persons or events that had become formative in the life of Israel for their understanding of who God is and what he does.

Analogy of Faith

This analogy is different from the analogy of antecedent Scripture that we have just visited. In the analogy of faith, we appeal to the discipline of systematic theology or doctrine to go through the whole Bible and pick up all the verses that pertain to a certain doctrine of the faith. Here we use a topical approach to our subject. Just as one would go out to the fields and pick various wildflowers to make up a bouquet, so in the analogy of faith the interpreter consults a concordance to find all the places where a theological term is used in the Bible, or one depends on systematic theologies to do the work of gathering. The verses are arranged into a single bouquet and presented as the teaching of the whole Bible on this topic. Interpreters must be careful to use this procedure only in their summary statements of the points claimed in a passage, lest the exegete fall into reading meaning into the text from teaching that is found elsewhere in the Bible. But once the meaning has been established in a text and the parallels are obviously there from teaching found in the whole of the Bible, we must not pretend that we do not possess the whole Bible. We must be clear in our methodologies to make sure that the meaning is really found and led out from the text rather than importing it into the text because something like it is taught elsewhere in the Bible.

Commentaries

Always try to determine what the passage teaches on the basis of the grammar and syntax of the text before going to commentaries. However, there is no need to claim omnicompetence or to pretend that the Holy Spirit has not worked among others who have studied this text. Therefore, choose two or three commentaries and let them talk to each other. Assess the relevancy and genuineness of their understanding of the text against the meaning of the words of the immediate context you are studying. Record the key concepts of each commentator, and show how they sometimes offset each other or how the text fails to support some of their claims. Then conclude with your own estimate on the same matters they have addressed.

Homiletical Analysis (page 7)

The time has come to put all of this together in such a way that listeners can hear in a fresh way the voice of God addressing them in their modern situations and lives. This will call for creativity, artistic skills, faithfulness to the text, and the process we shall refer to as the "principalizing" of the main points of the passage.

The Subject or Title of the Message or Lesson

Usually each passage has what we can refer to as a pivot point or focal point. This may be either a central verse that embodies the whole thrust of the passage or a climactic, memorable, or organizing clause or phrase that epitomizes the whole text under consideration. These words function as the fulcrum, or pivoting lever, for the whole passage.

It is this phrase, clause, sentence, or verse that will give us the best ideas for stating the subject or title for our lesson or sermon. The subject or title should be stated in such a way that it captures the attention of modern listeners. It also must be put in such a way that it is not merely a didactic statement or a truism about the past. One hint is to use in the title an "-ing" verb in order to communicate an exhortation that is in progress.

The Interrogative

One form of preaching and teaching is called the prepositional approach. It is a great aid in that it helps us to organize the teaching for each of the paragraphs, scenes, or strophes. It urges us to use one of the six interrogatives to determine what the passage is trying to do. We are to ask: "Is this passage answering the question who, what, why, where, when, or how?" Only one of these interrogatives can be chosen for each sermon or lesson. The way to do this is to take the subject or title that we have chosen and then to go down our block diagram/mechanical layout and ask for each of the paragraphs (or their equivalents), "Is this [insert the title of the message] about a who, what, why, where, when, or how?" One of these should answer the question more adequately than the other interrogatives.

The Homiletical Key Word

A perfect match for each interrogative is what we call a homiletical key word. This key word has three basic characteristics, all of which must be present. It must be: (1) a noun that names something, (2) an abstract noun, and (3) a plural abstract noun. The only noun that cannot qualify here is the noun "things." That noun does not name what it is that we have in mind to say; therefore, it must never appear. The noun used must be an abstract noun, for we wish to state principles that will be useful for our day. But since we are usually treating more than one paragraph, the noun must also be in a plural form.

Thus, to give some idea of how this works, when we find that the interrogative is "Why?" the homiletical key word will usually be "reasons." If the interrogative is "When?" we will have "times" or "situations." If it is "How?" the key word might be "ways" or "approaches."

The Main Points of a Passage

Each paragraph (or its equivalent) will result in a main point, or statement. Each of these statements will answer the interrogative in the way set by the homiletical key word chosen for that passage. The exegete must restate the themes of each of these paragraphs in the form of timeless, abiding truths that apply the ideas of the biblical writers faithfully while also applying these truths to the current needs of our world.

The Concluding Appeal

Every lesson or sermon should include one or two concluding paragraphs that issue a summons to action, a challenge to change, an appeal to the conscience, comfort for the present and future, or an indictment for unrepentant lifestyles. The question we should ask is this: "What is it that God wants us to do, say, or repent of, based on this text?"

As ambassadors of Christ, we beg persons to be reconciled to God. A good portion of our preparation must be devoted to praying through the text with a desire to make an appeal for action based on the text. All too often evangelicals are content to end the message with an appeal only to our cognitive skills. We ask our audiences to believe, to remember, to recall, all acts of cognition. But seldom have we thought through specific sets of actions that the passage calls for from all who hear it. Until God's Word has an action response, the preacher or teacher has not yet achieved the results that good teaching demands. May our Lord help us to help each other be more effective to the honor and glory of his name.

Appendix B

Biblical Integrity in an Age of Theological Pluralism

In my judgment, the most dramatic moment in the entire twentieth century came in 1946 when W. K. Wimsatt and Monroe Beardsley published their article "The Intentional Fallacy" in the *Swanee Review*.[1] This shot would eventually be heard throughout the century and around the literary world. Most of the careful distinctions this duo made have now been lost in the popular versions of their work, which are now understood to advocate something like this: Whatever an author may have meant or intended to say by his or her written words is now irrelevant to the meanings we have come to assign as the meaning we see in that author's text! On this basis, the reader is the one who sets the meaning for a text.

This astounding thesis changed all the rules of communication and interpretation. It gave the course for postmodernism, with its attendant methodologies, an enormous boost by setting a literary work free from its author's affirmations and thought and substituting instead a multiplicity of meanings that were imputed to the work by each and every individual reader! This has become the heart of the integrity issue as the twenty-first century now struggles to see if the word *integrity* has any meaning left for our day!

Reprinted, with changes, from *Evangelical Journal* 18 (2000): 19–28. Used by permission.

The fault with the previous generations, we were told by the postmodernist, was the "intentional fallacy," that is, the fallacy of depending on what an author meant to say by his or her own words as the real source of meaning in a text. On the contrary, the New Criticism bragged, meaning was to be found in the reader, or at the very least, in some merging of the horizons of the author and the reader, as Hans-Georg Gadamer tried to assert in 1960.

Gadamer's book *Truth and Method*[2] set forth the thesis found in the title of the book; namely, that truth cannot reside in a reader's attempt to get back to the author's meaning. This is an impossible task, for every interpreter has a new and different knowledge of the text in the reader's own individual, historical moment. Consequently, prejudice cannot be avoided, for the preunderstanding that one brings to the text colors his or her ability to arrive at any unified meaning of that text—much less the author's meaning of that text. Indeed, prejudice is to be encouraged, not denied, in the interpretation process. Anyway, the meaning of a text is indeterminate, so why act as if it were fixed? Meaning always goes beyond its author and is therefore a productive, not a reproductive activity. Only the subject matter, not the author, is the determiner of meaning. In the end, argued Gadamer, an explanation of a passage is never wholly the result of the interpreter's perspective or wholly that of the original historical situation of that text. It is instead the result of a "fusion of horizons" (German: *Horizontvershmeltzung*). Here the two perspectives become a third, new alternative and hence a new meaning. Furthermore, past meanings cannot be reproduced in the present, for the past, it was confidently asserted, cannot have presence or real status in the present. But what is all of this but a thinly disguised Hegelian dialectic of a thesis that is opposed by an antithesis, which results in a synthesis?

If the twentieth century was not reeling enough from Wimsatt's, Beardsley's, and Gadamer's theses from 1946 to 1960, more was to come in 1965 from Paul Ricoeur.[3] He too joined in the assault on the integrity of any written communication by demanding that a text be semantically independent from the intention of its author. A text would mean whatever it said to the mind of the reader, not necessarily what its author meant. Once a text was written down, its meanings were no longer determined by either the author or the understanding that the original audience had of those same texts. Each subsequent audience could read its own situation into a text, for a text, unlike talk, transcends its original circumstances. While these new meanings must not be completely contradictory to the original audience's understanding, they can be different, richer, or even more impoverished. In the end, Ricoeur set up the possibility for texts to open up a whole new world of meaning, since the meaning was no longer directly related to what was written, or at times even to the referent in that text. The new meaning was freed from the situational limits of meaning.

In the midst of this almost, by now, universal cacophony of voices, two lonely authors dared to buck the rush to assassinate the author: an Italian historian of law, Emilio Betti, and an American English professor at the University of Virginia, E. D. Hirsch. Hirsch first wrote in 1967,[4] acknowledging his debt to Betti's 1955 work in Rome.[5] Hirsch asked how we can validate the meanings we attribute to the texts we read. His answer was almost totally rejected by his generation—and even by some evangelicals. He dared to argue that verbal meaning is whatever an author wills to convey by any distinctive sequence of words. Moreover, he continued, the only genuinely discriminating norm for distinguishing valid or true interpretations from invalid or false ones is the author's assertions or truth-intentions. Thus, meaning is what is represented by a text; significance, on the other hand, names a relationship between that meaning and a person, concept, situation, or other things. The meaning of a text is fixed, but significance can and does change.

The polarities set up by the preceding names are those that have continued to dominate the twenty-first century. It is this issue, more than any other, that has given to us the crisis in literary integrity.

Biblical Integrity in Exegesis

The modern abandonment of the author as the determiner of the meaning of a text has had a radical effect on the textbooks that have been produced on biblical and literary interpretation in the last four decades. In a legitimate attempt to avoid the stultifying deadness and dryness of mere descriptive retelling of the biblical materials, in which the "then" of the b.c. or first-century a.d. historical context controlled the whole sermon, many have swung to the opposite extreme by making the reader sovereign over the meaning process. In this swing of the pendulum, so much emphasis today is placed on the "now," with an emphasis on the application or significance of the text, that little or no attempt is made to see if there is any connection between emphasized significance or application of a text and the meaning that the author intended.

But on what basis can an evangelical preacher or teacher fall for such a disjuncture and separation within the Word of God, thereby jeopardizing the divine authority of the text for God's people? The answer was not long in coming. For some evangelicals, it was located in two areas: (1) the practice of the Qumran community, which was attributed to the approximate time of our Lord Jesus, and (2) the alleged expansive and subjective practice of the New Testament writers in their citation of Old Testament quotations. The argument that is still widely accepted by evangelicals today, and which I believe is to the detriment of our movement and ultimately to the revered doctrine of an authoritative and inerrant Scripture, is that there is a surplus of meaning found in the Bible that goes beyond the understanding of the writers themselves. This surplus was put in the text by God apparently without the writers knowing it. God, who is the ultimate and divine author of Scripture, was able to put these additional meanings in the text in such a way that they eluded the human authors who originally wrote these texts under the inspiration of God. Accordingly, a dual authorship theory has developed in our midst that attributes the historical, grammatical, contextual meaning to the human author, while the deeper, spiritual, or applied meaning is to be found in what some call the *sensus plenior* meaning, or what others refer to as a *midrashic,* or *pesher,* meaning of the text.

How did we arrive at this state of affairs? It came in three waves. The first source of this emphasis was the Catholic writer Andrea Fernandez in 1925, who was the first to coin the term *sensus plenior* and to write on it. However, it was not until Father Raymond E. Brown completed his doctoral thesis in 1955 at St.

Mary's University on "The Sensus Plenior of Sacred Scripture" that the subject started to show up as well in evangelical circles some ten to twenty years later. Brown defined *sensus plenior* as "that additional, deeper meaning, intended by God, but not clearly intended by the human author, which is seen to exist in the words of the Biblical text . . . when they are studied in the light of further revelation or development in the understanding of revelation."[6] This view posited a double track of revelation: one that was on the surface of the text and a deeper one that was hidden, somewhere other than in the words, grammar, or syntax, in order that it might be discovered by later generations. Alternatively, it allowed later revelation (e.g., as found in the New Testament) to level out or equate to the same sense what earlier revelations had announced, but the basis for adjusting that new level of meaning was never defended. Neither was its textual evidence given, other than to say that all Scripture has the same divine author. Moreover, it was argued that if God is the ultimate source of revelation, he is free to impute whatever meanings he wishes, despite the semantic and linguistic restrictions that are usually found in the text.

The second wave came in a series of dissertations usually written for New Testament doctorates in the United Kingdom and focusing on the New Testament use of Old Testament quotations. The earliest of these was Earle Ellis's "St. Paul's Use of the Old Testament," but it was followed by several other dissertations. Common to most of these was the thesis that the New Testament writers often attributed to these older texts a new or additional meaning that could not be found in the surface meaning or in the grammar of the author's text. This matter was hotly contested by some in the seventies, eighties, and nineties, but others assumed that the statement was true since it came as the result of a number of doctoral theses.

The third wave that developed simultaneously with the second was the discovery of several commentaries among the Dead Sea Scrolls. The Qumran community practiced what was called a *pesher* type of exegesis, wherein contemporary values, persons, and situations were directly attributed as the exegetical values of the ancient persons and settings of the biblical text. Thus the "righteous" of Habakkuk 1:4 became the founder of the Qumran sect, their "teacher of righteousness." Likewise, in the Dead

Sea community's commentary on Habakkuk, the Chaldeans, or Babylonians, were transmuted into the contemporary Romans, who were threatening the Essene community.

All three movements converged in the second half of the twentieth century to line up with the now rampant movement of the abolition of the author from the interpretive process. Evangelicals did not agree with such an extreme action, of course, but they could evidence a sort of accommodationism that showed they were willing to argue for a multiplicity of meanings under certain conditions.

So, did the text evidence a deeper meaning that God had somehow hidden in the text until later generations suddenly discovered the dual-author theory of Scripture? Did the New Testament writers, as a matter of fact, exhibit a revelational stance in their alleged expansive use of Old Testament citations that showed that more was in the text than had met the eye in Old Testament times? And were the apostles and Jesus not only aware of such first-century interpretive methods as *pesher* and *midrash* that opened up new vistas of meaning, but have they also invited us to follow their alleged examples? Or did the apostles have a privileged revelatory stance, which allowed them to expand what could not be seen in the text, while under no circumstances are we to imitate their practices since ordinarily we are not recipients of revelation such as is found in Scripture? That is to say, could the apostles get so-called "deeper meanings" out of the Old Testament texts they cited, but we are not to follow their practice since they were given special ability to do this by virtue of their gift of revelation?

The Crisis in the Pulpit

Pity the poor pastor in the midst of all this diversity and pluralism! To whom can he or she go for an authoritative word from God? One option is to trust one's own instinct and to say that the deeper meaning one wishes to attribute to the text is the correct one, for he or she is a fellow believer who can sense the meanings that may not be immediately validated by an investigation of the grammar and history before us in the text. If such subjectivity is now allowed by the new rules of the game, then this is a whole lot better than the tedious work of teasing the meaning out of the text by working with the grammar, syntax, history, and theology of the Greek, Aramaic, and Hebrew texts. Another may decide that if the apostles could find such rich meanings in the Old Testament that would not have been advocated there by older methods of interpretation, then perhaps in the new age of the Spirit, this pastor could likewise apply a little "hermeneutical-stretcher" to similar texts. This would especially be understandable since the first-century community was probably exposed to such methods as *pesher* and *midrash*.

Despite all such rationalizations, O pastor or teacher, I urge you not to follow any of these methods. They are laden with serious pitfalls, with the ultimate calamity being the loss of divine authority for what is being communicated from the pulpit if one consistently applies these rules to the end. What is needed today is solid preaching of the Word of God in all of its extent (the whole counsel of God), in all of its assertions (paragraph after paragraph, chapter after chapter), and in all of its power (as written under the inspiration of the Holy Spirit)! To do anything less is like using a toy water pistol to put out a fire of secularism and paganism (and a host of other isms) that have engulfed the culture.

Loud protests are heard almost immediately, nonetheless. They complain, "But cannot God, the real author of Scripture, include a second meaning, which is unknown to the human author of Scripture?" That sounds spiritual enough, but is it? I contend that it is an inaccurate representation of the facts. God did not use the language of angels or the like but spoke to mortals in the language of the Greek marketplace and the tongue of the pagan Canaanites. Why? For one reason and one reason alone: In order to be understood!

If the argument is that part of the divine communication was to be subject to the normal rules of interpretation but another part was to be exempt from these constraints, then we must ask those who make this claim to show us which parts belong to which side and what the criteria are for making this division. And if it is further argued that the New Testament writers were given such a line of demarcation, enabling them to engage in such a bifurcating of the message, must we also assume, conceding momentarily the previous argument, that the number of passages that have this occult, or secondary, meaning is exhausted by the list of passages that the New Testament writers actually quote from the Old Testament? Or is this list merely suggestive, in which case our original request for the criteria must be answered? What is particularly difficult is to supply the criteria for this *sensus plenior*. Whatever else it is, it is not to be found in the *graphe*, what is written. But that, then, falls on hard times when it is realized that only what is written is inspired by God according to Paul in 2 Timothy 3:15–17.

The argument that God deliberately left a *hyponoia*, or an occult sense, in the biblical text to be deciphered later when the code would be cracked or revealed to selected, if not all, lay and clerical interpreters is a most audacious claim, to say the least. The very term "revelation" is one that shouts that God meant to "uncover," "to make bare" the meaning he had in mind when he spoke to his writers. To claim more or less is to take issue with God himself. There is not a shred of evidence for the presence of a secondary, mystical, or occult meaning, or *hyponoia*, lying in, around, or under the text. The burden of proof is on those who claim that such secondary senses and meanings are present to point where we are taught this truth in the biblical revelation itself. We ask only that they clearly spell out the criteria for locating the presence of such phenomena in the text and then give us the tools that we will need for unlocking these surplus values and meanings. Until then, we must basically interpret texts the way we interpret each other—that is, unless we wish all possibility of communication to cease!

The Crisis in the Seminary and the Church

What began as a crisis of epistemology and exegesis, wherein there was no place for absolute truth, much less for the authoritative Word of God, has spilled out into ever widening ripples of consternation. There has also been a crisis in the life of the church and in the seminaries, especially during the last three decades. Three dimensions of this crisis were outlined in Jeffrey Hadden's book *The Gathering Storm in the Churches*.[7] Hadden found a crisis of belief, of purpose (What is the mission of the church?), and of the orientation of the leadership of the church (a new class of church bureaucrats not closely connected with congregational life).

As the world of pluralism engulfed the church and seminary, the threefold loss mentioned by Hadden became more obvious. Seminaries lost their connection and identity as church institutions and tended instead to become freestanding centers of theological reflection and thought. All too often, with certain notable exceptions in the evangelical world, seminaries tended to accommodate their teachings to the culture of the post-Enlightenment world, often revising or just plain denying the faith the church had confessed in its past. Such accommodation was self-destructive to theology and ultimately to the very existence of the church itself.

James Turner's book *Without God, Without Creed* described this slippery slope in doctrine as well. He said:

> The crucial ingredient, then, in the mix that produced an enduring unbelief was the choices of believers. More precisely, unbelief resulted from the decisions that influential church leaders— lay writers, theologians, ministers—made about how to confront the modern pressures upon religious belief. Not all of their decisions resulted from long thought and careful reflection. . . . But they were choices . . . to defuse modern threats to traditional bases of belief by bringing God into line with modernity.
>
> . . . Put slightly differently, unbelief emerged because church leaders too often forgot the transcendence essential to any worthwhile God. They committed religion functionally to making the world better in human terms and intellectually to modes of knowing God fitted only for understanding this world.[8]

Turner thought that the second reason for the loss of focus was the seminary's embracing a multitude of causes, such as the environment and public policy issues. The seminaries became cause-oriented, with times that had previously been given to the study of biblical texts and theology now given over to a multiplicity of causes, many of which were flawed and doomed to die as time swept past its advocates. The gospel often was prostituted for parochial, flawed causes, especially those in which the seminary possessed no expertise: foreign policy decisions, economic and political platforms, and the causes of all sorts of groups claiming they had been made victims by the "system."

Turner's third reason for why the church had lost its roots and mission was the tendency for the seminary to run itself as if it were a graduate school or a mini-university. More often than not, the seminaries hesitated to teach from a position that affirmed certain verities of the faith and adopted instead a stance of taking students on a journey of the critical study of religion. Character and virtue development were no more a part of the calling of the seminary than was the professing and transmission of the faith once for all delivered to the saints. No longer was it assumed that a graduate from a seminary had read the Bible and was conversant with the main doctrines of the faith and its defense. Training in Greek and Hebrew were soon dropped from the curricula of many seminaries, as were courses in Bible knowledge and doctrine. In fact, even with such low expectations of seminary graduates, the situation grew worse when new faculty members arriving at seminaries no longer were expected, much less required, to have a seminary degree. The drift away from content and teaching of the faith devolved even further.

Some Long-lasting Effects of Pluralism

The resulting picture that has emerged as the church enters the twenty-first century is not an encouraging one at all. While evangelicalism has been insulated in some ways from the major impact of the loss of a determinate meaning in interpreting the Bible and the emerging pluralism of postmodernity, it too is susceptible to some of the same cultural forces that have been shaping many non-evangelical institutions. Barring a major revival and reformation of the evangelical movement, the evangelical church is likely to follow, even if at a delayed distance, the pattern already set by many who have made their peace with the contemporary culture and have accommodated it everywhere they could.

What has been conceded as an accommodation to the post-Enlightenment era? John H. Leith has given the most trenchant list of losses in his work about his own ecclesiastical tradition in *Crisis in the Church: The Plight of Theological Education.*[9] Here I present a modification and some reorganization of many of his points. The first great loss is the loss of church orientation as a result of university theological departments' stances and the church's secularization. Leith makes several points under this rubric that are well worth pondering. First, pay schedules that reward administrators significantly higher than professors with international reputations demonstrate that the seminary has followed a secular model and not that of the church. Second, campus life often is no different on a seminary campus than it is on a secular campus. Third, secular tenure policies undermine accountability to the church by insisting that professors whose teaching is out of tune with the life of the church still be retained, even if the church does not approve of it.

There is also the loss of a sense of mission and direction in many seminaries today. Any emphasis on evangelism, discipleship, missions, and catechism is likely to bring hoots of protest from many who regard such topics as beneath their dignity or calling in an academic center of study. Where are the encouragements for growth in the Christian life? They are found in all too few Christian universities, seminaries, and colleges.

Accompanying the above losses are two other features that are not healthy signs in this pluralist world. One is the loss of gratitude and accountability. Many of the long-standing institutions of higher learning were built out of endowments from God-fearing and Bible-loving donors who hoped for better things from these schools. But few today recall either the donors or their faith, much less are thankful to God for their sacrifice and vision. This absence of memory is critical, for it raises questions of morality as well as questions of direction. How could a wholly new set of purposes be substituted to contradict the purposes of those who built the institution? Leith almost assumes the role of an ancient prophet as he indicts the present leaders of these institutions by asking them how such distortions could be justified.

There is also a loss of real academic freedom as curriculum revision continues unabated. Whereas these schools once taught Bible, church history, theology (including ethics), and pastoral theology, many of these studies have been replaced with highly specialized fields of study, allowing little time for the mastery of a comprehensive view of the Bible and theology. Moreover, in an attempt to gain freedom *for* the study of the faith, the pendulum has already swung the other way with a cry for freedom *from* the faith. Academic freedom on a Christian campus is not easy to define. There must be freedom to study everything from every possible angle, yet for confessional communities it must be done within the context of the boundaries supplied by our faith. There never has been a community of study that is equally open to every possible idea; such an absolutist version is not possible even for a secularist who is committed to his or her own version of relativism, pluralism, or the like. Liberal theology can be very liberal when it comes to certain culturally agreed-upon dogmas of their own, but it is very illiberal toward those ideas it does not espouse. The orthodoxies of political correctness and certain "assured results of literary criticism of the Bible" leave no room for tolerance, despite the professed allegiance to pluralism and academic freedom.

Such losses cannot long continue without a crisis of major proportions taking place. Something must give in this state of affairs. Either the church will no longer recognize its scholastic offspring and the institution must become part of another mission/purpose statement, or the institution must take a hard look at what it has become, forsake some of the paths it is currently on, and adopt a whole new accountability to the church, its faith, and the authoritative role of the Scriptures.

The Conclusion to All of This

It is clear that when secular critiques of the theology departments and seminaries appear, such as Paul Wilkes's article in the December 1990 *Atlantic Monthly*, it is high time church people, Christian university and seminary administrators, and faculty begin to pay attention. But many within these schools have begun to set off alarms that a crisis is in progress. We have already referred to John Leith's *Crisis in the Church*, which describes the situation among Presbyterians. In the United Methodist Church, Geoffrey Wainwright of Duke University and

Thomas Oden of Drew University have been just as forthright in their analyses of the plight that is currently before the church and its seminaries or departments of theology. Robert Jenson and Carl Braaten have detailed the crisis in the Lutheran Church, and Christopher Seitz set forth a most interesting article on the Episcopalian Church in the June-July 1994 issue of *First Things*.[10] Evangelicals may not assume a smug air of superiority, for unless we take vigilant care, as sure as day follows night, many evangelical seminaries and churches will fall into the same traps.

Can nothing be done to prevent such a sad state of affairs within our own ranks? Of course! The first line of defense in the current debate is to insist that the author has a right to determine what his or her text must mean before anyone else says what that text means. This is critical. Should this battle be lost, the disastrous results of modernity and postmodernity are inevitable.

A second line of defense is the need to protect all endowment funds with a dissolution clause requiring the board of trustees of our Christian institutions to annually vote concerning whether the institution is still adhering to the doctrinal and purpose statements that were the basis on which the endowment gift was solicited. In the event that this should not be true, the board would be required to transfer those moneys to another group that is in agreement with such doctrinal statements and purposes.

The final suggestion for maintaining biblical integrity in the cultural wash of subjectivity, relativism, and pluralism is to institute closer forms of accountability to the church. All too frequently much emphasis is put on passing the accreditation standards of national or professional associations, but next to no attention is paid to an ecclesiastical evaluation. It would not be a bad thing if every five years each of the main divisions of the seminary theology department voluntarily invited segments of the ecclesiastical community to evaluate its goals, teaching, and processes as well as the students it was producing, just as the whole Christian university should invite a similar spiritual audit of its work. These written evaluations and the responses of the seminary would be available to potential donors and students as another guide in assessing whether a student should attend that institution and whether donors should continue to support the school with financial gifts and prayers.

It is time for a new partnership to be formed between the seminary and the church. Along with all the academic achievements, the seminary in particular must also demonstrate that it is just as vigilant about character formation, spiritual formation, and motivation of the school's products to serve and serve effectively before a watching church as well as a watching world. Only such devices as these will restore some of the loss of integrity that is all too rampant in both the seminary and the church.

Above all, the power of the Word of God must claim the place of primacy in the life of the church, seminary, and laity. Anything less will set us adrift with little or no chart or compass and no source of authority for life and thinking.

Notes

Introduction

1. John Bright, *The Authority of the Old Testament* (Nashville: Abingdon, 1967), 151.

2. Ibid., 92.

3. Elizabeth Achtemeier, *The Old Testament and the Proclamation of the Gospel* (Philadelphia: Westminster, 1973), 142.

4. Foster R. McCurley Jr., *Proclaiming the Promise* (Philadelphia: Fortress, 1974), 39; Donald E. Gowan, *Reclaiming the Old Testament for the Christian Pulpit* (Atlanta: John Knox, 1980), 4.

5. Gowan, *Reclaiming the Old Testament,* 13.

Chapter 1: The Value of the Old Testament for Today

1. See Walter C. Kaiser Jr., *Toward Rediscovering the Old Testament* (Grand Rapids: Zondervan, 1987), 26–32.

2. For those interested in the sermon outline just used from 1 Samuel 3, it is as follows:

Title: "The Power of the Word of God." Each of the four scenes in this narrative was made into a major roman numeral point, for it began in the previous days, went on to one night, then to the next morning, and finally it ended in subsequent days. Thus, there were four "characteristics" of that word: I. That Word Can Be Made Scarce for Us (v. 1); II. That Word Can Be Startling to Us (vv. 2–10); III. That Word Is Sovereign over Us (vv. 15–18); and IV. That Word Can Accredit Our Message (vv. 19–4:1a).

3. For confirmation and bibliography, see Alfred Edersheim, *The Life and Times of Jesus the Messiah* (Grand Rapids: Eerdmans, 1953), 2:710–41.

4. For a partial list and explanation, see Walter C. Kaiser Jr., *The Messiah in the Old Testament* (Grand Rapids: Zondervan, 1995).

5. Joachim Becker, *Messianic Expectations in the Old Testament,* trans. David Green (Philadelphia: Fortress, 1980), 50; see also p. 93.

6. Ibid., 93.

7. Ibid., 96.

8. James H. Charlesworth, "What Has the Old Testament to Do with the New?" in *The Old and New Testaments: Their Relationship in the "Intertestamental" Literature*, ed. James H. Charlesworth and Walter P. Weaver (Valley Forge, Penn.: Trinity Press International, 1993), 63.

9. Kaiser, *Messiah in the Old Testament*, 15–17, 78, 144.

10. Bernard W. Anderson, "The Bible as the Shared Story of a People," in *The Old and New Testaments*, 23–24.

11. I am indebted to my friend, Daniel Gruber in his book *Torah and the New Covenant: An Introduction* (Hanover, N.H.: Elijah Publishing, 1998), 5–13, for his organization of this concept that I have frequently mentioned in my own writings as well.

12. Ibid.

Chapter 2: The Problem of the Old Testament for Today

1. Emil Kraeling, *The Old Testament Since the Reformation* (New York: Harper, 1955), 8.

2. A. H. J. Gunneweg, *Understanding the Old Testament*, trans. John Bowden (Philadelphia: Westminster, 1978), 2.

3. For a fuller discussion of these matters, see Walter C. Kaiser Jr., *Toward Rediscovering the Old Testament* (Grand Rapids: Zondervan, 1987), 13–32.

4. For the best treatment of this theme, see Willis J. Beecher, *The Prophets and the Promise*, Princeton Seminary Stone Lectures for 1904 (Grand Rapids: Baker, 1972).

5. Bertil Albrektson, *History and the Gods* (Lund, Sweden: C. W. K. Gleerup Fund, 1967), 79.

6. The most definitive discussion of this problem of the passive form of the verb was given by O. T. Allis, "The Blessing of Abraham," *Princeton Theological Review* 25 (1927): 263–98. See especially p. 281, where he lists numerous examples of the passive meaning for the Hebrew *Hithpael* verb form, for this same verb form occurs twice later in Genesis in the passive form.

7. Martin Luther, *Commentary on Galatians*, trans. Erasmus Middletown (Grand Rapids: Kregel, 1976), 223.

8. *Ante-Nicene Christian Library*, Vol. 5/1, trans. A. Roberts and J. Donaldson (Edinburgh: T & T Clark, 1867), 313–14. I am indebted to Daniel Gruber for this citation in his *Torah and the New Covenant: An Introduction* (Hanover, N.H.: Elijah Publishing, 1998), 18.

9. Some laws of purification apply only to women, some govern the exclusion of lepers from the congregation, some apply to slaveholders, and some apply only to certain days or years.

10. A more advanced survey of the case made here is in Walter C. Kaiser Jr., *Toward an Old Testament Theology* (Grand Rapids: Zondervan, 1978). A less technical presentation of many of the same points in a popular form is Walter C. Kaiser Jr., *The Christian and the "Old" Testament* (Pasadena, Calif.: William Carey Library, 1999).

Chapter 3: The Task of Preaching and Teaching from the Old Testament Today

1. Emil Kraeling, *The Old Testament Since the Reformation* (New York: Harper, 1955), 8.

2. See Sidney Greidanus, *Preaching Christ from the Old Testament: A Contemporary Method* (Grand Rapids: Eerdmans, 1999).

3. Walter C. Kaiser Jr., *The Journey Isn't Over: The Pilgrim Psalms for Life's Challenges and Joys* (Grand Rapids: Baker, 1993).

4. Walter C. Kaiser Jr., *The Communicator's Commentary: Micah–Malachi*, ed. Lloyd J. Ogilvie (Waco: Word, 1992). It is now published as *Mastering the Old Testament: Micah–Malachi* (Nashville: Nelson, 1993).

5. Walter C. Kaiser Jr., *A Biblical Approach to Personal Suffering: Lamentations* (Chicago: Moody, 1982).

6. Walter C. Kaiser Jr., "Commentary on Exodus," in the *Expositor's Bible Commentary*, ed. Frank E. Gabelein (Grand Rapids: Zondervan, 1990), 2:285–497.

7. Walter C. Kaiser Jr., "Introduction, Commentary and Application of Leviticus," in *The New Interpreter's Bible*, ed. Leander E. Keck and David L. Petersen, et al. (Nashville: Abingdon, 1994), 1:983–1191.

Chapter 4: The Art and Science of Expository Preaching

1. I have argued more fully for this definition and methodology in my book, *Toward an Exegetical Theology: Biblical Exegesis for Preaching and Teaching* (Grand Rapids: Baker, 1981).

2. Ronald J. Allen, *Preaching the Topical Sermon* (Louisville: Westminster/ John Knox, 1992), 2.

3. Sidney Greidanus, *Preaching Christ from the Old Testament: A Contemporary Hermeneutical Method* (Grand Rapids: Eerdmans, 1999), 203–77.

4. Ibid., 227–28.

5. Ibid., emphasis added.

6. Gordon D. Fee and Douglas Stuart, *How to Read the Bible for All It's Worth: A Guide to Understanding the Bible* (Grand Rapids: Zondervan, 1982), 26.

7. Karl A. G. Keil, *De historica librorum sacrorum interpretatione ejusque necessitate* (Leipzig, 1788); idem, *Lehrbuch der Hermeneutik des neuen Testamentes nach Grundsatzen der grammatisch-historischen Interpretation* (Leipzig: Vogel, 1810). This latter Latin work was translated in an English text in 1811 by Emmerling.

8. See the exceptional discussion of the grammatical-historical interpretation by John Sailhamer, "Johann August Ernesti: The Role of History in Biblical Interpretation," *Journal of the Evangelical Theological Society* 44 (2001): 193–206.

9. Ronald Allen, "Shaping Sermons by the Context of the Text" in *Preaching Biblically*, ed. Don Wardlow (Philadelphia: Westminster, 1983), 29–30. Soon after came Thomas G. Long, *Preaching and the Literary Forms of the Bible* (Philadelphia: Fortress, 1989).

10. The chapters of the Bible were not divided off until fairly recent times. The Archbishop of Canterbury, Stephen Langton (A.D. 1150–1228) is usually given credit for dividing the Bible into its present chapter divisions.

11. Allen, *Preaching the Topical Sermon*, 2.

Chapter 5: Preaching and Teaching Narrative Texts of the Old Testament

1. Don Wardlow, ed., *Preaching Biblically* (Philadelphia: Westminster, 1983).

2. Robert Scholes and Robert Kellogg, *The Nature of Narrative* (London: Oxford University Press, 1966), 240.

3. J. P. Fokkelmann, *Narrative Art in Genesis: Specimens of Stylistic and Structural Analysis* (Amsterdam: Van Gorcum, 1975), 9.

4. Sidney Greidanus, *The Modern Preacher and the Ancient Text: Interpreting and Preaching Biblical Literature* (Grand Rapids: Eerdmans, 1988), 199.

5. Shimon Bar-Efrat, "Some Observations on the Analysis of Structure in Biblical Narrative," *Vetus Testamentum* 30 (1980): 165.

6. Of course the focus is twofold here, for it could just as easily have been, "Identifying the Man of God."

7. Richard G. Bowman, "Narrative Criticism: Human Purpose in Conflict with Divine Presence," in *Judges and Method: New Approaches in Biblical Studies*, ed. Gale A. Yee (Minneapolis: Fortress, 1995), 29–30.

8. Robert Alter, *The Art of Biblical Narrative* (New York: Basic Books, 1981), 182.

9. Ibid., 74–75.

10. Ken Matthews, "Preaching Historical Narrative," in *Reclaiming the Prophetic Mantle: Preaching the Old Testament Faithfully*, ed. George L. Klein (Nashville: Broadman, 1992), 37–38.

11. Alter, *The Art of Biblical Narrative*, 95–113.

12. Bar-Efrat, "Some Observations," 155.

13. I am indebted to Ken Matthews for pointing out this otherwise well-known example in his "Preaching Historical Narrative," 38–39.

14. Meir Sternberg, *The Poetics of Biblical Narrative* (Bloomington, Ind.: Indiana University Press, 1985), 186.

15. See John W. Welch, "Introduction," in *Chiasmus in Antiquity*, ed. John W. Welch (Hildesheim: Gerstenberg, 1981), 11.

16. Dale Ralph Davis, *Looking on the Heart: Expositions of the Book of 1 Samuel* (Grand Rapids: Baker, 1994), 1:47–48.

Chapter 6: Preaching and Teaching the Wisdom Books of the Old Testament

1. Fred B. Craddock, *As One Without Authority* (Nashville: Abingdon, 1971), 25–26.

2. John C. Holbert, *Preaching Old Testament: Proclamation & Narrative in the Hebrew Bible* (Nashville: Abingdon, 1991), 37–38.

3. This definition is alleged to have come from Cervantes. It is quoted in James Creshaw, *Old Testament Wisdom: An Introduction* (Atlanta: John Knox, 1981), 67.

4. Brevard Childs, *Old Testament in a Canonical Context* (Philadelphia: Fortress, 1985), 211–12, as I was reminded by Duane A. Garrett's citation in his "Preaching Wisdom," in *Reclaiming the Prophetic Mantle: Preaching the Old Testament Faithfully*, ed. George L. Klein (Nashville: Broadman, 1992), 109.

5. Walter C. Kaiser Jr., *Toward Rediscovering the Old Testament* (Grand Rapids: Zondervan, 1987), 178–79. See also John Bright, *The Authority of the Old Testament*, 2d ed. (Grand Rapids: Baker, 1975), 136.

6. I am indebted for much of what follows here, though in my own revised and reworked form, to Alyce M. McKenzie, *Preaching Proverbs: Wisdom for the Pulpit* (Louisville, Kent.: Westminster/John Knox, 1996), 4–9.

7. McKenzie, *Preaching Proverbs*, 6.

8. Duane A. Garrett, "Preaching Wisdom," 116–17, and idem, *The New American Commentary: Proverbs, Ecclesiastes, Song of Songs*, ed. E. Ray Clendenen (Nashville: Broadman, 1993), 123–28.

9. Garrett, *The New American Commentary*, 172, n. 363.

10. See for further detail, Walter C. Kaiser Jr., *Ecclesiastes: Total Life* (Chicago: Moody, 1979).

11. The Hebrew text uses the shortened name of God here—"Yah." Some English translations treat the divine name as if it were an intensifying adjective or adverb. This is without strong grammatical support.

12. For further development of this passage, see Walter C. Kaiser Jr., "True Marital Love in Proverbs 5:15–23 and the Interpretation of Song of Songs," in *The Way of Wisdom: Essays in Honor of Bruce K. Waltke*, ed. J. I. Packer and Sven K. Soderlund (Grand Rapids: Zondervan, 2000), 106–16.

Chapter 7: Preaching and Teaching the Prophets of the Old Testament

1. See Gary V. Smith, *Prophets as Preachers: An Introduction to the Hebrew Prophets* (Nashville: Broadman and Holman, 1994), who analyzes the prophets with a view to showing how they attempted to transform the peoples' responses by using current theory on how people think.

2. William L. Holladay, *Long Ago God Spoke: How Christians May Hear the Old Testament Today* (Minneapolis: Fortress, 1995), 186.

3. Claus Westermann, *Basic Forms of Prophetic Speech*, trans. Hugh Clayton White (Louisville: Westminster/John Knox, 1991), 98–118.

4. See Walter C. Kaiser Jr., *The Christian and the "Old" Testament* (Pasadena, Calif.: William Carey Library, 1999); idem, *Toward an Old Testament Theology* (Grand Rapids: Zondervan, 1978).

5. Claus Westermann, *Prophetic Oracles of Salvation in the Old Testament*, trans. Keith Crim (Louisville: Westminster/John Knox, 1991).

6. For a more detailed analysis of Isaiah 40 and a discussion of a sample sermon preached on this text, see Walter C. Kaiser Jr., "Our Incomparably Great God," in *Inside the Sermon: Thirteen Preachers Discuss Their Methods of Preparing Messages*, ed. Richard Bodey (Grand Rapids: Baker, 1990), 171–84.

Chapter 8: Preaching and Teaching the Laments of the Old Testament

1. Hermann Gunkel, *The Psalms: A Form-Critical Introduction*, trans. Thomas M. Horner (Philadelphia: Fortress, 1967).

2. Joachim Begrich, "Das priestliche Heilsorakel," *Zeitschrift fur die alttesta-mentliche Wissenschaft* 52 (1934): 81–92.

3. Delbert Hillers, *Lamentations: The Anchor Bible* (Garden City, N.Y.: Doubleday, 1972), xxxiv.

4. Karl Budde, "Das hebraische Klagelied," *Zeitschrift fur die alttestamentliche Wissenschaft* 2 (1882): 1–52. See also W. R. Garr, "The Qinah: A Study of Poetic Meter, Syntax and Style," *Zeitschrift fur die alttestamentliche Wissenschaft* 95 (1983): 54–75.

5. This suggestion was put forth by Paul W. Ferris Jr., *The Communal Lament in the Bible and the Ancient Near East* (Atlanta: Scholars Press, 1992), 10. Ferris defined a communal lament as "a composition whose verbal content indicates that it was composed to be used by and/or on behalf of the community to express both complaint, and sorrow, and grief over some perceived calamity, physical or cultural, which had befallen, or was about to befall them and to appeal to God for deliverance."

6. This concept of depth coming by constructing acrostics was suggested to me in an article by John Piper, "Brothers, Let the River Run Deep," *The Standard* 72 (1982): 38.

7. Samuel Cox, *The Pilgrim Psalms: An Exposition of the Songs of Degrees* (London: R. D. Dickinson, 1885), 17. See also Walter C. Kaiser Jr., *The Journey Isn't Over: The Pilgrim Psalms for Life's Challenges and Joys* (Grand Rapids: Baker, 1993), 21–30, for a full exposition of Psalm 120.

8. Used by permission of Rev. Dr. Dorington G. Little.

9. Captain Elliot Snow, *Adventures at Sea in the Great Age of Sail: Five First-hand Narratives* (New York: Dover, 1986), 1–104. Originally published as *The Sea, the Ship, and the Sailor* (Salem, Mass.: Marine Research Society, 1925). Captain Barnard's own engaging and revealing title of his account is "A Narrative of the Sufferings and Adventures of Captain Charles H. Barnard, in a Voyage Around the World, During the Years 1812, 1813, 1814, 1815 & 1816; Embracing an Account of the Seizure of His Vessel at the Falkland Islands, by an English Crew Whom He Had Rescued from the Horrors of a Shipwreck; and of Their Abandoning Him on an Uninhabited Island, Where He Resided Nearly Two Years."

10. Psalms 50, 73–83.

11. Alexander MacLaren, *The Book of Psalms: 39–84*, in *The Expositor's Bible* (New York: A. C. Armstrong and Son, 1902), 376.

12. Note the cohortatives used here in the second of each pair of verbs, "*I shall . . .*"

13. Abraham Heschel, *God in Search of Man* (New York: Farrar, Straus, and Cudahy, 1955), 98.

14. Derek Kidner, *Psalms 73–150* (London: InterVarsity, 1975), 280.

Chapter 9: Preaching and Teaching Old Testament Torah

1. See J. T. Burtchaell, "Is the Torah Obsolete for Christians?" in *Justice and the Holy: Essays in Honor of Walter Harrelson,* ed. D. A. Knight and P. J. Paris (Atlanta: Scholars Press, 1989), 113–27. Also see Walter C. Kaiser Jr., "Images for Today: The Torah Speaks Today," in *Studies in Old Testament Theology,* ed. Robert L. Hubbard Jr., et al. (Grand Rapids: Eerdmans, 1992), 117–32.

2. The argument for this translation is found in Walter C. Kaiser Jr., *The Messiah in the Old Testament* (Grand Rapids: Zondervan, 1995), 42–46.

3. See this confirmed in Claus Westermann, "The Way of Promise Through the Old Testament," in *The Old Testament and the Christian Faith,* ed. B. W. Anderson (New York: Harper and Row, 1963), 208–9.

4. Gerhard von Rad, *The Problem of the Hexateuch and Other Essays* (New York: McGraw-Hill, 1966), 1–26.

5. For a summary of those challenges, see H. B. Huffmon, "The Exodus, Sinai, and the Credo," *Catholic Biblical Quarterly* 27 (1965): 102–3, nn. 6–10.

6. H. C. Schmitt, "Redaktion des Pentateuch im Geiste der Prophetie," *Vetus Testamentum* 32 (1982): 170–89. Schmitt's article was pointed out to me by my former colleague, John H. Sailhamer, "The Mosaic Law and the Theology of the Pentateuch," *Westminster Theological Journal* 53 (1991): 241–61.

Chapter 10: Preaching and Teaching Old Testament Praise

1. Hermann Gunkel, *The Psalms: A Form-Critical Introduction,* trans. Thomas M. Horner (Philadelphia: Fortress, 1967).

2. The NIV renders the word "autumn rains" (Ps. 84:6), but the older texts translated it as "teacher." The Hebrew words for "rain" and "teacher" are spelled almost exactly the same way except for one vowel, which, of course, was not in the original text but was added later. Also see Joel 2:23 for the same translation problem between Hebrew *moreh* ("autumn rains") and *morēh* ("teacher").

3. Some of the Old Testament texts where *'El Hay,* "living God," appears are: Ps. 42:2; Josh. 3:10; Deut. 5:26; 1 Sam. 17:26, 36; Isa. 37:4, 17; Jer. 10:10; 23:36; Hos. 1:10; Dan. 6:26.

4. See also Deut. 33:29 and Ps. 115:9.

Chapter 11: Preaching and Teaching Old Testament Apocalyptic

1. See the introduction in John J. Collins, "Apocalypse: The Morphology of a Genre," *Semeia* 14 (1979): 5–8.

2. The verbs in the Hebrew text are what are usually called *waw* consecutives with the imperfect form of the Hebrew verb. This pattern appears frequently in narratives. While we are not always as certain as we would like to be in translating other Hebrew verbs, this form is the only one that is consistently translated everywhere else as a past "tense" verb. It is not clear why the NASB and the NIV rendered the four verbs in the future tense.

3. See Walter C. Kaiser Jr., *Back toward the Future: Hints for Interpreting Biblical Prophecy* (Grand Rapids: Baker, 1989), 51–60. Also see Walter C. Kaiser Jr., "Hermeneutics and the Theological Task," *Trinity Journal,* n.s., 12 (1991): 3–14.

Appendix B: Biblical Integrity in an Age of Theological Pluralism

1. W. K. Wimsatt and Monroe Beardsley, "The Intentional Fallacy," *Swanee Review* 54 (1946); reprinted in William K. Wimsatt Jr., *The Verbal Icon: Studies in the Meaning of Poetry* (New York: Farrar, Straus, 1958), 3–18.

2. Hans-Georg Gadamer, *Truth and Method: Elements of Philosophical Hermeneutics*, translated and revised by Joel Weinsheimer and Donald G. Marshall (New York: Seabury, 1975; reprint, Crossroad, 1982).

3. Paul Ricoeur, *Interpretation Theory: Discourse and the Surplus of Meaning* (Fort Worth: Texas Christian University Press, 1976).

4. E. D. Hirsch Jr., *Validity in Interpretation* (New Haven: Yale University Press, 1967).

5. The most accessible work of Betti is Emilio Betti, *Die Hermeneutik als allgemeine Methodik der Geisteswissenschaften* (Tubingen: Mohr, 1962), translated and reprinted in Richard E. Palmer, *Hermeneutics: Interpretation Theory in Schleiermacher, Dilthey, Heidegger and Gadamer* (Evanston, Ill.: Northwestern University Press, 1969), 54–60.

6. Raymond E. Brown, "The *Sensus Plenior* of Sacred Scripture" (S.T.D. diss., St. Mary's University, 1955), 92.

7. Jeffrey Hadden, *The Gathering Storm in the Churches* (Garden City, N.Y.: Doubleday, 1969).

8. James Turner, *Without God, Without Creed* (Baltimore: Johns Hopkins University Press, 1985), 266–67, as cited by John Leith, *Crisis in the Church: The Plight of Theological Education* (Louisville: Westminster/John Knox, 1997), 41–42.

9. Leith, *Crisis in the Church*, 13–24.

10. Christopher Seitz, "Pluralism and the Lost Art of Apology," *First Things* (June-July 1994): 15–18.

Glossary

allegorize. A type of interpretation that suggests that a deeper meaning is present than the one found on the surface in the ordinary rendering of a text of Scripture.

allegory. An allegory is a metaphor (involving an unexpressed comparison) that extends beyond a single word or sentence to a story so that spiritual, moral, or other abstract meanings are represented by actions or characters that serve as symbols of more than the surface meaning.

analogy of antecedent scripture. The method of interpreting the Bible in which careful note is taken of the use of special terms that have acquired meaning in the history of revelation, of all direct and indirect references or allusions to previous persons, events, or citations, and of the contents of the covenants. This will form an "informing theology" that accumulates expanded significance as revelation continues to build on what has been revealed in the past.

apocalyptic. A genre of the biblical text that derives its name from the Book of Revelation, which in Greek is *Apokalypsis*, meaning a "revelation," or an "uncovering." This form is found in the latter half of the Book of Daniel and sections of Isaiah and Zechariah. It is marked by a strong emphasis on the future, the presence of angels, dreams, and symbols.

colophon. A colophon is a tailpiece. It comes at the end of a work and either identifies the title, author, and date of a work or gives a literary finishing touch to the work.

ennead. A set of nine, or as it is in Isaiah 40–66, sets of nine chapters.

equational proverb. This is also sometimes called a *synonymous parallelism*. It is a proverb in which the second half, or line, of the proverb says in different words the same thing as the first half of the proverb. (The formula is: A equals B; or where there is A, there is B.)

genre. A literary type or a form of a composition or section of the Bible.

inaugurated eschatology. A description of the future work of God in which an announced future event has both a "now," or current fulfillment, and a "not yet," or distant future realization. Both are seen as part and parcel of one single idea of what God is doing and will do in the distant future.

isogogics. Isogogics, or biblical introduction, is the area of biblical study that is devoted to answering questions regarding the age, authorship, genuineness, and canonical authority of the various books of the Bible.

metaphor. A metaphor is an implied or an unexpressed comparison between two different objects. (The formula is: A is B, without using the words "like" or "as.")

metonymy. A figure of speech in which there is a change or a substitution of one name for another in order to give it a force and impressiveness it otherwise would not have.

oppositional proverb. This is sometimes called an *antithetical parallelism.* It is a proverb in which the second half, or line, of the proverb says the opposite of the first half of the proverb. (The formula is: A does not equal B; or better A than B.)

proverb. A condensed parable consisting of riddles, enigmas, similes, and metaphors. Rather than being confined to a single word, it expresses a comparison of similitude in a sentence or more that is short and pithy. It embodies a certain kick to its expression, which is memorable, and is usually located in some key happening.

rib. A Hebrew word meaning a "lawsuit" wherein Yahweh usually appeals to a jury of the heavens and the earth to listen to his case against Israel in their failure to follow God.

rubric. A title or heading for a literary work. Originally it was written in red, hence its derivation from the archaic word for "ruby," or "ruddy."

simile. A formal comparison made between two different objects. The use of the words "as" or "like" generally tip the interpreter off to the presence of this expressed comparison. (The formula is: A is as/like B.)

Sitz im Leben. A German expression meaning the "setting in life," that is, the historical, cultural, real location in space and time that a Bible passage has.

Sitz im Literatur. A German expression meaning the "literary setting" that a passage has within a body of literature as opposed to its "setting in life."

textual criticism. This is the discipline that has as its special object the task of ascertaining the exact words of the original texts of the sacred text of Scripture.

Subject Index

allegorical interpretation, 43, 45

Big Idea, 55

context
  book, 180–81
  canonical, 180–81
  immediate, 181
  section, 180

Edict of Constantine, 36
eisegesis, 12, 49
Enlightenment, 44
expository preaching, 49–50, 53, 59

final appeal, 50, 59
focal point, 55
fusion of horizons, 191

genre, 12, 53
golden calf, 18
gospel
  meaning of, 25
  in the Old Testament, 42
grammatical-historical method, 10, 52

Hebrew language, 39
homiletical analysis
  final appeal, 188
  homiletical keyword, 187
  interrogative, 187
  main points, 188
  title of the message, 187
hyponoia, 197

intentional fallacy, 191
interrogative, 56–57

lament
  communal, 125
  individual, 123
  representatives of, 123
law(s)
  ceremonial, 23
  civil, 23
  moral, 23
  narrative framework of, 141–43
  relation to faith, 143–44
  relation to promise, 140–41
  versus grace, 34–35

main points, 57
megachurch, 10
messiah, 20–23
midrash, 195, 196
mitte of the Old Testament, 30
modernity, 41
music, 10

narrative
  characterization, 69–70
  dialogue, 71–72
  leitwort, 73
  plot, 66–67
  point of view, 67
  rhetorical devices, 74–77
  setting, 79–71
  scene, 64–66
  structure, 73–74

one meaning, 10–12
Old Testament
    practical usefulness of, 40
    size of, 41

pesher, 195, 196
pericope, 54, 56
pluralism, 199–201
postmodernism, 11
post tenebras lux, 19
promise-plan of God, 24, 31, 32–34
prophet(s)
    call of, 19
    dreams of, 17
    foretellers, 111
    forthtellers, 111
    lawsuit genre, 110–11
    oracles against foreign nations,
        111
    woe oracles, 110
    words of judgment, 102–7
    words of salvation, 107–10
    validation, 20
praise psalms
    declarative, 153, 154–55
    descriptive, 153, 154
proverbs
    clusters of, 89–90
    equational proverbs, 87
    genre of, 84

metaphor in, 88
metonymy in, 88
oppositional proverbs, 87
simile in, 88

reader response, 44
reading the Bible backwards, 26, 28

Scripture authors
    call of, 16
    preparation of 16
sensus plenior, 197
subject of a passage, 56
syntactical analysis
    block diagramming, 183
    literary type, 181
    paragraphing, 182
    topic sentence, 182

theology
    of the holy, 23
    of marital love, 23
    of suffering, 23
theological analysis
    analogy of antecedent scripture,
        185
    analogy of faith, 185–86
    key theological terms, 184–85

unity of the Bible, 31, 37

Author Index

Abegg, Martin G., Jr., 47
Achtemeier, Elizabeth, 11
Albrektson, Bertil, 32, 46
Allen, Ronald, 50, 53
Alter, Robert, 71, 72–73
Averbeck, Richard, 21

Barnhouse, Donald Grey, 50
Beardsley, Monroe, 191
Becker, Joachin, 21
Begrich, Joachin, 121
Bergen, Robert D., 46
Betti, Emilio, 193
Bonar, Andrew, 80
Bowman, Richard, 68
Braaten, Carl, 203
Bright, John, 10, 11
Brown, Raymond, 194–95
Budde, Karl, 122

Calvin, John, 19, 77–78
Charlesworth, James H., 22
Childs, Brevard, 85
Craddock, Fred, 83

Davis, Dale Ralph, 80
Delitzsch, Fredrich, 36

Ellis, Earle, 195

Fee, Gordon, 52
Fernandez, Andrea, 194
Ferris, Paul W., Jr., 210
Fokkelmann, J. P., 64

Gadamer, Hans-Georg, 192
Garrett, Duane A., 46, 90–91
Gowan, Donald, 11, 12
Greidanus, Sidney, 50–51, 65
Gunkel, Hermann, 121, 153
Gunneweg, A. H. J., 30

Hadden, Jeffrey, 50–51, 65
Hansen, Paul D., 46
Hewitt, C. M. Kempton, 46
Hillers, Delbert, 122
Hirsch, E. D., 193
Holbert, John C., 83

Jenson, Robert, 203

Kaiser, Walter C., Jr., 45, 46, 47, 179, 180
Keil, Karl A. G., 52
Kent, Dan G., 46
Kraeling, Emilio, 29, 39

Leith, John H., 200
Little, Dorington, 129
Luther, Martin, 34

MacLaren, Alexander, 133
Marcion, 36, 39, 43
Martens, Elmer A., 180
Matthews, Kenneth A., 45, 73
McCurley, Foster R., Jr., 11
McKenzie, Alyce M., 46, 86–87

Oden, Thomas, 203

Philo, 43
Pratt, Richard L., Jr., 46

Rad, Gerhard von, 142
Ricoeur, Paul, 192
Robinson, Haddon, 55

Sandy, D. Brent, 47
Schmitt, H. C., 143–44
Seitz, Christopher, 203
Smith, Gary V., 46
Sternberg, Meir, 75

Stott, John, 50
Stuart, Douglas, 52

Tenney, Merrill, 178
Turner, James, 199–200

Wainwright, Geoffrey, 202
Ward, Christine, 46
Ward, James, 46
Wardlow, Don, 53, 63
Willke, Paul, 202
Wimsatt, W. K., 191

Scripture Index

Genesis

1–2 40
1–11 141
1:22 142
1:28 142
2:4 75
2:15–17 72, 75
2:18 97
3 40
3:1–2 72, 75
3:15 33, 108, 140
5:1 75
5:2 142
6:9 75
8 112
9:1 142
9:27 108, 140
10:1 75
11:10 75
11:27 75
11:27–25:11 74
12 42
12–50 141
12:1 143
12:1–3 140, 142
12:2–3 33
12:3 32, 38
15:1 160
15:6 29, 143
15:7 142
15:9 143
17:1 143
22 42, 66, 70, 73
22:2 143
25:12 75
25:19 75
25:23 141
26:2 143
27 67
31:3 143
35:11 143
36:1 75
36:9 75
37 73
37–50 74
37:2 75
37:31 73
37:33 73
38 73
38:17 73
38:25–26 73
43–45 74
49:9 88

Exodus

2:24 141
3:6 141
4:5 143
14:31 144
19:3–8 142
20 34, 40, 145
20:2 142
20:2–17 142
20:4 156
21–23 145
25–40 145
25:9 145
25:40 145
32:25 78, 176
34:25 18
16:1–34 146–52
18–20 145
23:27 150
23:32 150

Numbers

1–10 145
12:6–8 101
14:11 144
16 156
20:12 144

Deuteronomy

1:32 144
5 40, 145
9:23 144
12:32 27
13 26
18 26
22:8 144
25:5–9 142
32:43 38

Joshua

6 104
24:16–18 142

Judges

2:1 35, 108
9:7–15 92
14:14 92
17:6 75
18:1 75
19:1 75
21:25 75

1 Samuel

1–6 74
2:27–29 80
3 65
3:1 18, 65
3:1–4:1 77–82, 205 n. 2
3:2–14 19, 66
3:15–18 20, 66
3:19–4:1 20, 66
9:2 69

2 Samuel

7 22, 33, 73
22:50 38

219

1 Kings

8:33–50   124
17   65, 67, 74
17:1   66
17:2–7   66
17:8–16   66
17:17   105
17:17–24   66
17:24   67, 71
17–2 Kings 13   74
18   74
18:27   77
19   74

2 Kings

1:9–15   72
2:14   74
14:9   92

1 Chronicles

6:33–37   156
9:17–19   156
9:23   156
25:1–5   156

2 Chronicles

3:1   70

Job

1:13–19   74
5:17   93
12:1   77
12:2   93
14:2   93
16:13   93
16:19   93
23:1–7   93
28   93
31   93
41:1–5   93
42:7   93–94

Psalms

1:2   143
2   154
3–7   123
5:12   160
7:1   124
7:3–5   124–25
10–14   123
13:1   124
15–28   123
16   22

16–17   123
18:49   38
19:7–11   143
22–23   123
29   154
30   155
31   123
34   155
34:1–9   155
35–36   123
35:13   150
38–43   123
42   156
43   156
44   123
45   154
46   155
48   154
51–59   123
60   123
61–64   123
65   155
67   155
68   123
69   123
71   123
72   154
73   123
73:13   124
73:21–22   133
74   123
77   123
77:1–20   129–38
79   123
80   123
82   123
83   123
84   154
84:1–12   156–60
84:6   211 n. 2
85   123
86   123
87   154
88   123
89   123, 154
90   123
92   155
100   154
100:1–5   154
102   123
106   123
106:15   19
107   155
109   123
109:8–10   125
109:30–31   125
110   22, 154
115   123
116   155

117:1   38
118   155
119   143
120   123
120–134   47, 154
120:1–7   128–29
120:2   124
130   123
132   154
135–136   154
138   155
145–150   154

Proverbs

1:8–9:18   91
5:15–23   94
6:20–35   90, 91
6:27–28   90
7   98
10:15   88
11:1–21   89–90
11:22   88
12:19   88
14:4   87
15:16   87
15:17   88
19:16–23   90–91
19:20–21   90
20:13   87
21:2   87
22:17–24:22   90
25–31   90
25:14   88
25:15   88
26:14   88
29:18   18, 78, 82, 176

Ecclesiastes

1:2–2:26   93
2:24   93
3:1–5:20   93
5:18   93
6:1–8:15   93
7:1–29   92
8:15   93
8:16–12:7   93
9:13–16   92
12:1–7   92
12:9–14   92

Song of Solomon

1:2   98
4:12   97
4:15   97
8:6   98
8:6–7   94

Isaiah

1–5   16
5   110
7–12   111
10:1–11   110
11:10   23
13–23   111
24–27   111
28:1–4   110
29:1–4   110
29:15   110
30:1–3   110
31:1–4   110
40   40
40–48   103, 181
40:1–2   113
40:6–8   113
40:12–31   113–18
41:21–29   111
48:22   103, 181
49–57   103, 181
52:13–53:12   40
55:10–11   81
57:21   103, 181
58–66   103, 162, 181
58:3–5   150
63   123
64:24   103
65–66   40, 112

Jeremiah

1:4–5   16
5:18   108
11   123
14   123
15   123
17–18   123
18:7–10   112
20   123
23:28–29   17
25:1   166
25:12–14   166, 168
29:10–14   166, 168
31:31–34   33, 35
32:36–44   108–10
44:1–6   106
44:7–30   106–7
46–51   111

Lamentations

1:2   126
1:4   126
1:7   126
1:8   126
1:11   126
2   128

2:1–22   127–28
2:11   126
3   123
3:4–5   122
3:24   126
5   126

Ezekiel

25–32   111

Daniel

4:16–25   169
4:32   169
7–12   162
9:2   166
9:20–27   166–72

Hosea

12:4   42

Joel

1:13–14   163
2:12–14   163
2:18–19   163
2:19–27   164
2:23   211 n. 2
2:28–31   22
2:28–3:21   164
3:1–21   164–66

Amos

1–2   103, 104, 111
3:1   103
3:1–5:17   104
4:1   103
5:1   103
5:18   103
5:18–6:7   110
5:18–6:14   104
6:1   103
7–9   104
7:1   103
7:4   103
7:7   103
8:1   103
8:11–12   18, 79, 178
9:1   103

Jonah

2   155

Micah

1–2   103
1:2   103
2:1–4   110
3–5   103
3:1   103
6–7   103
6:1   103
6:1–8   111

Habakkuk

1   123
1:4   195
2:6–19   110

Zechariah

12–14   162
14   40
14:20   169

Malachi

1:1–5   181
1:6–2:9   181
2:10–16   181
2:17–3:6   181
3:7–12   181
3:13–4:6   181

Matthew

1   27
5:6   158
5:17   35
5:19   35
6:21   87
24:15   171

Luke

13:32   88
24   24
24:25–26   24
24:25–27   41

John

5:39   23
5:46–47   26

Acts

2:16–36   22
2:42   173
3   22
3:18   22

4:12   30
6:7   173, 174
7   22
9:31   174
12:24   173, 174
13   22
13:32–33   33
13:49   173, 174
15   34
16:5   174
19:20   173, 174
20:27   44, 178
24:14   27
26:6   27
26:22   27
28:23   27
28:31   174

Romans

1:1–2   42
3:31   35
4:15   34

5:13   35
7:7   34
8:31   136
9–11   25
9:4   25
9:11–12   141
11:29   25
11:33   25
12:15   127
15:9–12   38

1 Corinthians

15:3–4   27

Ephesians

4:32   177

Philippians

4:2   177

2 Timothy

3:14–17   84
3:15–17   198
3:16   17
3:16–17   40

Hebrews

1:1–2   102
3:17–4:2   42
6:18   42
7:27   151

1 Peter

1:3–12   31
1:10–12   41

1 John

2:18   161
3:2   161